This is one of those books that you read,
and then have to sit back or curl up in a ball and
"be still and know."

In these honest, tear-stained pages are clear
signs that there is a "Hound of Heaven" hunting us
down—this Spirit that is stalking us with love,
winking at us with miracles, tickling us with
grace, subverting everything that could
destroy us, and whispering in our ears that
we are truly beloved.

—Shane Claiborne
author, activist, recovering sinner
www.thesimpleway.org

Reluctant Pilgrim

**A Moody, Somewhat Self-Indulgent Introvert's
Search for Spiritual Community**

Enuma Okoro

FRESH AIR BOOKS®

Nashville

The Fresh Air® Web site http://www.freshairbooks.org

Fresh Air Books® is an imprint of Upper Room Books®. Fresh Air Books® and design logos are trademarks owned by The Upper Room®, a ministry of GBOD®, Nashville, Tennessee. All rights reserved.

Cover and interior design: Marc Whitaker/www.mtwdesign.net
Cover photo: Julia Parris
Typesetting: PerfecType, Nashville, TN

LIBRARY OF CONGRESS CATALOGING-IN-PUBLICATION DATA
Okoro, Enuma, 1973–
   Reluctant pilgrim : a moody, somewhat self-indulgent, introvert's search for spiritual community / Enuma Okoro.
      p. cm.
   ISBN 978-1-935205-10-4
1. Okoro, Enuma, 1973– 2. Christian biography. 3. Spiritual biography.
4. Religious biography. 5. Church. I. Title.
   BR1725.O48 2010
   277.3'083092—dc22
   [B]   2010028922

Printed in the United States of America

To
All my girlfriends,
in their white lab coats,
gorgeous shoes, and steel cases
of oxygen

and

in memory of
Clark Michael Rivinja

Always . . .

"Let the wild rumpus start!"

Maurice Sendak
Where The Wild Things Are

Contents

Acknowledgments

Thank you, Clark, for believing in me and in my writing abilities from the very get-go. You always said I could do it and that you'd always be there to support me in any way you could. And you have been there, even now. I know how proud you would be, and I know somehow you'll find a way to read this book, even if it's over someone's shoulder. Thank you for making me a better, stronger, and more caring person. I miss you every day, but at least now I know heaven is a funnier place with you there. Please don't make Jesus watch that one *South Park* episode where he's in the boxing ring.

Thanks to my family—I love you, Mom.

Thanks to my editor Kathleen Stephens, at Fresh Air Books, for her patience, her patience, and her patience. Thanks to Amy Lyles Wilson for stepping in and seeing me through. Sarah Arthur, thanks for being my steadfast writing buddy and super-encourager. You made writing look so easy that I actually thought maybe I could do it too! Shame it's not as easy as it looks, huh? Thanks to Jenny Howell my heart friend. You are there for me in countless ways and always. Thank you, Lisa Yebuah, for just being in my life. You are my sister. Lissa Smith—far away friend and constant cheerleader, #16 on my bucket list—yes, I am secretly and openly in love with you (smile)! Carole Baker, thanks for being there through the years. And thanks to my friend Jonathan Tran. I just want your name in here somewhere in case you're ever famous. Actually, I should probably put Fred Bahnson's name in here too. He's gonna be famous someday also. Remember guys,
I knew you when!

And finally, thank you to my growing church community, the Reverend Greg Moore and All Saints' United Methodist Church in Brier Creek, Raleigh, North Carolina. You are teaching me to see the face of Christ and, God help us, to perhaps be that face on occasion.

Part One

Shifting Sanctuaries

(All names have been changed to pig latin
to protect the identity of people.)

Chapter 1

My Father's Child

Sunday morning
You were always there, usually
sitting beside me
at Mass, everything
was quiet between you two and I
could get lost in the awe
of my surroundings.
Didn't you hold my hand
during prayers,
when we walked in and out
of sanctuary spaces
didn't you buy me crucifixes
and rosaries,
Never even questioning why . . .
I dreaded Sundays
Like any child forced awake.
But I loved riding
with you in the car,
holding hands in the pews,
Sunday's best Daddy
And me your little girl.

Reluctant Pilgrim

I started writing poetry about my father after he died unexpectedly a few years ago. It was the only way I knew how to process my grief. And somehow those poems began to hint at my relationship with God. My heart seems constantly entangled with threads that tether me to the holy. I have always lived close to sanctuaries. In my mind's eye I cannot picture my first sense of home without imagining God just a stone's throw away. The first house I remember was in Queens, New York, kitty-corner from the Catholic Parish of my baptism, Saint Nicholas of Tolentine. Within a few years we moved directly across the street from a synagogue, and I found out that God lived in more than one place. I had my first lemonade stand outside that house by the synagogue, and at the end of the day my father bought all my leftover lemonade and drank my minor accomplishment down, Dixie cup by Dixie cup. He was the first saint I fell in love with, and for better or for worse I didn't learn saints were fallen until much later. When I was seven, he decided that the family should move back to West Africa. He wanted his four children to have a firm sense of Nigerian identity. In his opinion we were becoming far too Americanized. That was one of the many things my parents fought over. But on Sunday mornings the only real point of conflict was how late we were running for Mass. My father was as punctual as a full stop. My mother was not. She was as fragmented as the last sentence with lots of loose ends.

Like most families, we all had our acquired roles. My older brother was affectionately known as a mama's boy, a comedic introvert trying to navigate his adolescence amidst the emotional, high-strung inflammatory zone of his three sisters. He had no choice really but to do as we did and said; otherwise, he could find himself wrestled to the ground, stripped down naked, and rolled up in a carpet runner as one of us read aloud his diary and broke the secret that he was in love with Jaclyn Smith from the hit TV show *Charlie's Angels*. For the most part he was an obedient only boy.

My older sister was the firstborn, the overly opinionated rebel constantly looking far into the horizon for ever more lines to cross. If trouble broke out, the best guess was that she either started it or instigated one of us to start it. And my little sister was the baby—in my eyes, the brat, the apple of my mother's eye, and the hypersensitive one with skin thinner than wasp wings. I, on the other hand, was communally regarded as my father's favorite, bookish and always off somewhere by myself writing songs or reading the encyclopedia or the dictionary. I was also the little seven-year-old girl who collected crucifixes and had to slide over siblings to slip into the pew next to my father, holding his hand all through Mass.

Once we moved back to West Africa, I was introduced to my first mosque, and the rest of my early childhood was lost in a whirling dervish of Hail Marys and muezzin cries to holy prayer. I was raised by a Catholic father, an Anglican, somewhat evangelical mother, and endless Muslim aunts, who called on both Jesus and Allah within the same breath, depending on the circumstances. I ran into God beneath the billowing skirts of Catholicism and Islam while learning the cultural steps of being a foreigner in my native country. When people ask me where I'm from, I fumble for answers, take a deep breath, and exhale with, "I was born in the States, but my parents are Nigerian, and I grew up in four different countries. But currently I live in (insert current city of residence) so that's where I'm from, I guess."

Eventually, I end up telling the whole story, about living in Nigeria and the Ivory Coast into my early teens, attending boarding school in England, and having family throughout America and in various African and European countries. I grew up never living in one place for more than three years. Identity has always been somewhat of an issue for me. As the third of four children and from an extended family comparable in size to Jesus', I learned early in life to burrow out my own niche in new environments, stake my territory, and get to work rearranging the furnishings of my internal life as necessary.

My faith story isn't any less complicated. My religious education was parsed out in doses of Roman Catholicism washed down with long gulps of multiflavored Protestant theology.

I had a pretty privileged upbringing. I don't have a tragic story to tell you about how the church wounded me in my childhood and then twenty

years later I stumbled into a chapel hidden in a New York alley because the choir was singing a hymn that made me think of my dead mother baking biscuits after service when I was growing up in a trailer park on the edge of town before I ran away after the organist touched me inappropriately. I will admit to you off the bat that I am a drama queen, but none of that kind of stuff has happened to me. No, I am just a regular person trying to live my regular life. Except that my regular life largely includes being a Christian who doesn't really like church or many of the people I find in church. The even trickier part is I'm also a Christian who believes that Christ calls us to live in the community of the church and to love our neighbors. So things have been kind of sticky most of my adult life. I am a well-raised, charming, highly educated young woman who can get even a mute person to tell me her or his entire life story in less than an hour. But that doesn't mean I know about neighborliness and servanthood. It basically says I know how to work a room. Working the kingdom of God, on the other hand, is a whole other story.

The truth is I don't know much about Christian community—what makes one tick, how to break into one, how to commit to one, or why Christ considered belonging to one so essential. And I can't figure out whom to blame: the churches I've walked in and out of for the past decade or me, myself, and I? Methinks it a complex question I have raised, but I am willing to point all fingers at all the various churches whose doors I've graced in the past five to ten years. But that wouldn't be completely fair— mostly true but not 100-percent fair. So let me confess a few things about myself. I have always been somewhat of a solitary figure, a moody person who gets nervous when I start to feel my personal space threatened by too many people or activities or hard-and-fast requirements like job responsibilities, paying my taxes on time, and sending Christmas cards. As a result, I like to call the shots, to say when I am available and for how long. I panic at the thought of having to be somewhere and having to spend time with people I don't know nor have a vested interest in. Trying to get a commitment out of me for something as nonthreatening as lunch on a certain day that is not today is like trying to extract a splinter with a Q-tip.

Because after all, what if I'm not in the mood to talk on that afternoon, or if I'm in the middle of writing something brilliant, or if I'm just caught up in something else? I just don't know how I'll feel on that day at that time that you are trying to get me to commit to knowing about right now. I love to read and I love to write and I love to spend countless hours imagining how much better my life is going to be in the future. Such passionate pursuits often happen best when I am alone. So my life is quite solitary, and I often suffer from acute loneliness, but I can't bring myself to imagine that giving up control of my time would reap better benefits. I know I have issues. But that's not the worst part.

The worst, and possibly scariest, thing about all this is that, like I said earlier, before I had any say in it, I was claimed as a Christian. Whether or not others might call me a Christian is up for grabs, but I belong to a faith tradition formed and steeped in the idea of self-denial for love of the neighbor and rooted in community. Just by the nature of my baptism I am part of a distinct and storied community whether I like it or not, whether I acknowledge it or not. I belong to a tradition that tells me my life is not really my own but rather is caught up in the divine and communal life of something much bigger than myself. I am a character in a story I did not write, and there are many other characters in addition to myself who are equally important. But these are all tenets I find hard to swallow on a daily basis. I prefer the parts of the tradition that talk about grace and God's forgiveness of us and the fact that none of us can ever really measure up to perfection. These parts offer me the illusion that I am off the hook from striving to be something I obviously was not cut out to be—holy.

I am not proud of these personality quirks. In fact, I often desperately wish that I were more of the other kind of person—open to people, hospitable, self-sacrificing, and sharing—possessing all those ingredients that contribute to the community potluck. I imagine that if I were that kind of person, I'd have to gamble less on God's graces getting me into the pearly gates. (Which, after all, is what this is all about anyway, right?) But the other type of person, the grace-gambler type, is who I have discovered myself to be.

Reluctant Pilgrim

On most Sunday mornings I'd rather be sitting with a coffee cup in one hand and the *New York Times Book Review* in the other than sitting in a church pew with a hymnal or bulletin. Getting myself to church is usually what happens when the Lilliputian-sized angel on my right shoulder sweet-talks her way into my conscience and I give in yet again to the "trust me, you'll like it" speech. Do I end up liking it? Sometimes. But most times I strive to convince myself that worshiping God isn't necessarily about liking it as much as it is about doing it because it goes with the territory of having been created by God. Is there something to be said for going through the motions even when it comes to worship and faith? I think I heard a seminary professor say that once, and he said it with such authority that I figured it had to be true. I'm not so sure. I'm still thinking about it. I *want* to like worshiping God. I *want* to like engaging those spiritual disciplines that thousands of people before me have done through the centuries. But I'm getting ahead of myself. I want to go back to what I was saying about my story earlier.

It's a faith story that revolves around Jesus Christ, the man born in first-century Palestine, who I believe was actually God of all time and space. I've been gathering pieces of the story since I was a little girl, since I could parse out words. No one has asked me why I stay a Christian if I seem so naturally averse to some of the major components. I wish someone would ask me so I could say it is because I have not given up hope that I, like the rest of humanity, am indeed redeemable. And I would also add something about mystery and baptism.

But before any of that I would say this: *I am not like Jesus.* And in various sundry circumstances I would not want to know what Jesus would do because honestly, I am pretty certain it is not what I would want to do. In fact, if I owned a sweatshop *my* various cheap accessories would say WWED: *What would Enuma do?* because, honestly, that's more or less how I live my life, at least the daily minutiae of my life. And I think this is somewhat troubling because the Bible says that Jesus is into minutiae—stray hairs count. Don't worry, this will be a story about my spiritual journey, but I feel the need to make this early confession so that you, the reader,

Enuma Okoro

can read, knowing that I, the writer, have laid my spiritual cards on the table. I'm not sure how much further along I am on my faith journey than when I was eight years old sprawled out on the living room floor reading the big children's Bible. I'd like to think I've grown by leaps and bounds since then, that I'm on to the solid food Saint Paul mentioned once. At least now I know the order of the Gospels: Matthew, Mark, Luke, and John. And I can tell you in which chapter of Matthew to find the Sermon on the Mount. And I know that Jesus was Jewish not Christian. I do know some things. But I struggle with some other aspects of the faith I profess to follow. I'm not terribly good at feeding the poor (umm, because most of the time I think I am the poor) or visiting prisoners or caring for widows and orphans. I never have prostitutes over for dinner (unless they're family), as a self-employed writer I'm a little bitter about tax-collectors, and I don't even know any Samaritans, let alone the good ones. So basically I often think I'm screwed.

All this sort of came to a head seven years ago, once I walked out the doors of a renowned theological institution with a degree in my hands. I didn't immediately feel more equipped to engage the world with my trained understanding of how *the perichoretic dance of the Trinity is more metaphysical than a tangible reality.* What does that even mean, people? Nor was I any more in love with the church or anymore convinced that I needed a regular and consistent church community to help me be more faithful to Jesus. The sad bottom line was that after seminary I realized I still didn't get the half of it. I hadn't found a home church in several years. My most fervent prayer was still about finding a hot godly man with really thick hair. I had no clear or bold sense of vocational direction, and I could barely remember what I had spent three years learning. Furthermore, I still loved designer shoes and handbags and I would hands-down pick a spring jaunt to visit museums in Paris over a Habitat Mission trip to Tegucigalpa, Honduras. Did Jesus care that I had found my new camel-colored Marc Jacobs hobo bag for a third the price (no, it's *not* a knockoff) as much as he cared about how many deflated soccer balls could fit into a backpack headed for the border? That's a tough question. So I covered my bases and

lived a double life of mission leader/Parisian tourist for several years. In fact, sometimes I packed the deflated balls in my designer luggage.

Needless to say, I walked out of those divinity school doors realizing that I still had questions to ask myself in order to locate a sense of authenticity. I did not seem to be the Christian who veered toward intentional community, who ranted and raved for reconciliation, who felt called to solidarity with the marginalized, or who couldn't wait to have my very own congregation. I was more of what I like to call a fine-print Christian. The general points were easily recognized and communally affirmed, but the fine print on my redemption contract had clauses for most everything. Seminary did not turn me into the kind of Christian I thought I should be. Rather, in the face of my peers it helped me own up to the kind of Christian I am—right or wrong or more likely somewhere in between. I was awed by and grateful for my seminary colleagues who felt compelled to share their homes with multiple families, friends, and strangers, or who read Mennonite theologian John Howard Yoder and enlisted in radical nonviolent peacekeeping teams that acted as human shields in war-torn countries. No doubt Jesus was a radical. Me, however, not so much.

I needed to ask what certain words meant to me, words I had taken for granted but that now had to bear real definitions for me. I felt compelled to understand them in order to make better sense of my faith: *baptism, hospitality, witness,* and a slew of others. While becoming theologically educated, new words like *beauty, creativity,* and *delight* had seeped into my language of faith, and I needed to think through their compatibility with the more traditional words. In a bizarre way, these spiritual mind games pushed out the stained-glass walls I'd built around God and offered me a bigger and broader sense of who God might be and who exactly could fill out an application to join that royal priesthood that Saint Peter talks about in 1 Peter 2:9.

So clearly if I write anything about my spiritual journey, it's not going to be about how I grew into this wise, self-sacrificing woman of God. (Though if that's what you come away with, fine.) My spiritual story is going to be about how faith can be scarring and yet beautiful all at once.

It's going to be about me finding bits and pieces of God's grace the more I realized just how unlike Jesus I actually am. It's going to be about my rocky on-again, mostly off-again love affair with the idea of church, and the painful process of learning that *community* and *church* are not always synonymous. And somehow throughout all this I'll tell you about my deep love of God and my often conflicting attempts to understand Christian community and to live as though I could indeed recognize the kingdom of God if it kicked me in the ass. I might also tell you about my love of reading, of poetry, of art, of good-looking men with permanent jobs, and other things that somehow affect my faith. I'll find a way to make the necessary connections, and I'll pray that by the end of this story you are not praying for my salvation while waiting in line for your money back. That being said, here goes.

Chapter 2

Bridegroom of the church,
forgive me when I fail to see you even amidst the
cracks of a broken and complicated church.

I have a confession to make. Being on the sidelines at church is beginning to grow on me. There are a lot of really smart people on the sidelines and we get to talk about all sorts of things. Yes, I am assuming that I am one of the smart people. Don't judge me, you don't even know me yet. Like I was saying, there are good conversations on the sidelines. Once, we, the smart people, huddled together and talked about how if Jesus came back, we bet he wouldn't even recognize the church anymore because it's full of overprivileged consumers who have no idea what real faith costs. We knew we were true witnesses to be able to say such things aloud in a place like Starbucks. Maybe someone would overhear us and get curious enough to want to learn more about Jesus. Yes, I am writing all this tongue in cheek, but it's true, all of it, I swear. Especially the part about being on the sidelines.

It may seem strange to think that I have spent most of my adult life terribly in love with God and equally at odds with the idea of church. I can't even blame my disdain for the church on a rigid Catholic upbringing. I happen to love the Catholic Church more or less, the way you still love a childhood best friend you haven't seen in years. She never did me wrong. She introduced me to a God I fell in love with and that's got to count for something. When I was a child I was in awe of everything church-related, from the oversized figure of a crucified Christ to the velvet pouches on sticks that came round during the offering. I used to imagine taking off the deep purple velvet pouches from their sticks and using them as little purses. Growing up in cathedrals, I always thought of the physical space of the church as a place where beauty met the holy. All that colored glass reflecting sunlight, the rows of ornate wooden pews, the velvet kneeling benches, the stone and marble. God had an awesome sense of feng shui. I still could sit in cathedrals all day long. But these days, with my penchant for sitting around with friends eating good food and drinking cheap wine, I'd rather be hosting dinner parties in those beautiful rooms with the vaulted ceilings and not kneeling on the pews.

For most of my adult life I have struggled to find a church that feels like home, or even just a place where I might bump into Jesus on my way to the bathroom. He'd be wearing a toga with "J-Unit" printed on the front. I'd give him the peace sign, he'd give me the "What up" head nod, and we'd both walk back into the service, not even trying to outpace each other so we didn't feel awkward. Maybe I'm conjuring up a Christ with whom I feel I could be my broken-edged self, with whom I could sit in the pew, and in the middle of the prayers, lean over to and whisper, "Okay, maybe the idea of church isn't sooo bad, but what's really supposed to be going on here? Should I feel as unseen as I do in these places? Am I scared of what a good and faithful church would ask of me? I don't know because so far church just feels like a vague concept I'm supposed to automatically understand. But the reality of it has been a big disappointment. You know I love you, J-Unit, right? I want to try and figure this out, and I want to want to come to church but most of the churches I've been to suck. So what now?"

I don't know what exactly he'd say, but I think he'd pat my knee and tell me we were going to get through this together and that maybe after service we could go grab some coffee and I could start to tell him more about what I've been experiencing and he'd promise to listen for a while before making any comments. Then I'm pretty sure he'd tell me to quit talking during the prayers and to stop calling him "J-Unit."

✳ ✳ ✳

I can't pinpoint the day when church became a place where I felt invisible—where I could walk in and out on recurring Sundays and feel like no one knew anything about me, where the same people might ask me my name again and again, where as a single woman there was no comfortable niche to slide into. It brings tears to my eyes just thinking about some of those Sundays, of pulling into the church parking lot and mentally and emotionally gearing myself up to walk into the sanctuary alone, a stoic mask of protection shadowing my face and my posture. I would walk in determined not to feel awkward or self-conscious of being alone or of not knowing anyone. I'd sit through the service antsy for the Eucharist, so I could slip out right after receiving. I don't even remember when I stopped having expectations of feeling either seen or welcomed or even having a desire to meet and greet anyone. At some point, church became a means to an end—getting the Eucharist and nothing else, except maybe hearing the sermon if the preacher was any good. I had resigned myself to being in church without having any sense of community or belonging.

At one particular church I attended on and off for about a year, the person I spoke to the most and who knew my shoddy attendance habits best was a sexton named James. He would catch me sneaking in one of the side entrances right before the lectionary readings, and he'd whisper to me, "Good morning, lady. Running late again?" I'd smile sheepishly and look guilty. James always stood in the back or just outside of the side aisle and he'd help me look for an inconspicuous seat that allowed easy access and exit. Sometimes when weeks would pass without my attendance, he'd greet me the next time with "Hey, stranger, where you been?" And he'd always leave me with, "See you next week?" James was the only person I felt any loyalty to in that congregation of over a thousand people. But that's not to say people ignored me. No, no, no. Though it's hard to want to engage someone when it's clear right off the bat that they are going to see what they want to see about you and rarely anything more—usually because it would be too much work, as mutual life-giving relationships have a habit of being. One woman, learning I was from Nigeria, shook her head and offered the heartfelt and neatly packaged comment, "Isn't

it horrible about AIDS there." I wanted to ask her if she thought it was horrible about AIDS here. But maybe I'm being too judgmental. Another time, at the onset of the Easter service where I happened to be wearing an outfit native to Nigeria, the woman standing next to me started a conversation, introducing herself as an important so-and-so on some important board of trustees. Her introduction was quickly followed with enthusiastic questioning: "Where are you from?" she gushed, "You look just like a princess in your beautiful African costume." I didn't have the heart to tell her that the "costume" I was wearing was almost twenty years old and a hand-me-down of my mother's that I had easily talked her out of because she thought it was only suitable to wear to the market. If my mother knew I had worn that outfit to Easter Sunday service, I would have been called a few things before "princess." Again, I might be reading too much into things, but eventually, instead of trying to change my attitude, I just stopped going. I've thought about popping my head in there one Sunday just to let James know I'm all right but I won't be coming back.

When I talk with other people about feeling somewhat out of place in church, it seems that many have a hard time talking about going to church without getting worked up in some way or another. And those who don't get worked up can't seem to offer any compelling reason why I should go to church. "Because that's what Christians do" has never been enough for me. It's almost like people of my generation bought a ticket for a spiritual journey back when we were in college, and now fifteen years later we're ready to get off the train, kind of like overdoing a backpacking trip through Europe. You've seen and experienced a heck of a lot, you know you've been changed, but it is all a bit exhausting and you're still somewhat wondering if you found what you were looking for in the first place. Except now you're getting too tired to care. You're a bit frustrated that after all this traveling time you still don't really understand the local idiosyncrasies and idioms. That's what going to church feels like to me sometimes—a backpacking Eurotrip that's lost its lure and mystery. And yet I surprise myself in conversations with people who clearly have deep opinions against church. Suddenly I find myself articulating all the reasons why church is a necessity for any serious disciple committed to growth. It's sort of like the whole "It's my family so I can knock it but don't you dare start in!"

The truth is, I'm still in shock that I'm actually admitting this, confessing that being a part of the church has been a real struggle for me. My self-proclaimed reputation as a spiritual guru, a twenty-first-century mystic, a divine-like being with an amazing sense of style who seemingly chose God over the Parisian runway is on the line. But the other reason I'm finding this sharing so hard is because I haven't told you everything. I haven't mentioned that there's a small part of me, let's call her Tiny E, who senses there's a whole other world through that mythical church door that seems so small to me. Maybe I have to convince myself to drink the cup so that the big self with all the answers gets cut down to size a little, and Tiny E can go through the small door and join the madness that seems so foolish to me right now. I don't know. But I'm going to have to tell you about a whole lot of things before I figure that out.

Chapter 3

Father of all creation,
make your imprint on my heart, so that your image
is the standard by which all others are seen.

In my father's house there were many rooms, and for almost a year he kept our places prepared because he could not believe that we were not coming back. He used to tell me over the phone from Nigeria that all my things were still in my room, waiting for me. When he did eventually pack up our toys and our clothes that we had left behind, he put them in the storage room at the back of the house. That was twenty-five years ago. But if my father were alive I know my things would be there.

The only two letters my father ever wrote to me sit in the top drawer of my bedside table. One is from 1984, a year after we left him, and the other is from 1987—a sentimental response to a harsh, indicting letter I wrote to him when I was fourteen years old. Twenty-one years ago. These are the only tangible pieces of him I have. That and the engagement ring he gave my mother, which fits only on my wedding finger. I forget the letters are there except for every once in a while when I chance upon them. Sort of like certain pictures and voices from my past. I forget they are there, almost like secrets told me so long ago that I have forgotten I can now conjure them up and tell them.

* * *

I am good at keeping secrets. When I was nine years old I kept a secret from my father. I didn't tell him that his family was coming apart at the seams and that his world was about to be changed forever. That might also have been the year I learned it can be difficult to breathe and to love at the same time. I can never forget him standing there by the departure gate in the Lagos airport. He is waving good-bye as his wife and four children board the plane for our vacation in America. I still remember what it felt like watching him from the end of the airplane ramp, trying to get my wave just right so he wouldn't guess we were really leaving. I was treading water in an undercurrent of danger and the threat of being found out flooded my little heart and drowned out any immediate feelings of loss or betrayal. No comment was safe and no gesture thoughtless, until the airplane door locked firmly in place. I knew my father wasn't perfect, but I worshiped him anyway. Of all his children, I was his favorite. I knew it. He knew it. They knew it. He thought he was sending us on a four-week vacation while he stayed behind to work. He didn't know that more than half of us were not returning. He would have to wait a month and read about it in the letter my twelve-year-old brother would bring back with him on the plane.

My mother had told us a few weeks earlier that when we packed for this supposed vacation, we needed to pack anything we wouldn't want to leave behind because some of us would not be returning. She was leaving her marriage of sixteen years and planning to keep the younger two of her four children with her. My older brother and sister were settled in their respective boarding schools in Nigeria and so would remain under my father's care. Providing for my sister and me was all my mother could afford to do, and to this day I don't know how she did it. I only know what she tells me, that she felt she needed to get out of her marriage for the future of her life and her children. I don't blame her, because I can never know all that she experienced in her marriage. What I do know is that my mother probably bore more sacrifices for her four children than she's ever let on. What I tell, I know from the perspective of a child.

For those few weeks before our trip I had to be extra careful about how I talked to my father, lest I let slip about our adventure. If he asked me why I was taking so much with me, I had to reply that I couldn't bear four weeks without my precious toys. I am uncertain to what extent I fully realized that my mother's ticket to freedom was cradled in tiny hands. So I began to pack, selecting my future with the fumbling palms of a nine-year-old. I had a very special cream-colored vanity case, the old carry-on kind shaped like a rectangular box. Mine was a hand-me-down from my mother, and while she packed our clothes and necessities, it was my special task to pack my vanity case. I do not remember how I sealed up my little West African world into that small carry-on. But I did. I chose what was going and what was staying. I left behind my red-and-white-checkered school uniform. I left behind my Richie Rich comic book collection that my father had helped me accumulate. I left behind my Don Williams country music tape but took my Diana Ross and the Supremes *Greatest Hits.* I left behind my stack of songs that my fourth-grade girlfriends Helen and Lola and I had written after school, camped out on my living room floor still wearing our checkered dresses.

One thing I clearly remember taking is a little jewelry box. It was my most prized possession—a four-inch-wide square box with a white plastic flip-up mirror top that had "Hello Kitty" etched into it. It was burnt on one corner where a childhood experiment with candles and matches had left its mark. In the bottom half of the box, red with two small drawers, I kept my fourth-grade treasures—a tarnished aluminum ring with a smiley face and puffed up eyes that jiggled when you shook it, a silver tinted blue rosary with only forty-eight beads held together by a safety pin where the other two beads had fallen off, and one of my dad's old cuff links I'd salvaged when he threw it away. And that is all I remember out of everything I took.

After that vacation, I lost years with my father that I can never reclaim. Our visits became more infrequent as my little sister and I grew into our teens and as our parents' relationship became even more strained. But I thank God for the resilience of children. I have fond memories of the nine years we were a family, however broken and damaged and disillusioned. I had nine years of knowing what it was like to be a family, with my siblings and me as soldiers in the trenches of our parents' war. My sisters and brother and I looked out for each other and took our respective turns

at the front lines, leaving the others to rest in the abundantly grace-filled dugouts of childhood we could find. And there were times of cease-fire between my parents. Times when both seemed to try so hard to be kind and gentle to each other, moments when we really were that family going to the club on Sundays after church, where my parents would play tennis while we would swim in the pool with my cousins, playing Marco Polo, feeling around for one another, laughing and flailing our arms in our self-imposed blindness.

* * *

I don't remember which came first, falling in love with God or falling in love with my father. But my place at his side was assumed and unquestioned, like my little sister's place at my mother's side and my two older siblings' somewhere in between us all. I don't know why I started collecting crucifixes, but part of what I remember about the excitement of going to Mass each Sunday was that after the service, local peddlers would lay out their religious wares on colorful Nigerian ankara cloth outside the Ikoyi Catholic Church gates—trinkets and amulets to sustain the faithful on the days between holy visits. On spiritual impulse you could pick up plastic opalescent rosaries, glossy snapshots of Mother Mary in gold-rimmed picture frames or crucifixes carved of wood, melded in silver or refined in gold. It was church market—clearly the kind that wasn't unbiblical. I would beg my parents on a regular basis for some memento, some cute minute replica of a dying Christ to take home with me. And that's where my father started buying me Jesus. Those are the clearest memories I have of my childhood faith. When we left Nigeria, I left the Catholic Church as quietly as I left my father, without questions or explanations, too young to understand the lines being crossed but sensitive enough to know the story was barely beginning.

Chapter 4

Omnipresent God,
you play hide-and-seek with me so that I might
strive and strain for you and rejoice when I find
you. Have mercy upon me.

"Soooo, if I was baptized as an infant and like didn't really have any say or like any idea what I was getting into with this whole baptismal calling stuff, does that mean that I'm like still called into the work of God?" I sat in the back of the lecture hall, listening with gaping mouth as a fifteen-year-old girl in a tight-fitting tee shirt with sparkly letters that said "You Don't Know My Name But Your Boyfriend Does" astutely asked a question. The professor replied with an equally thought-provoking answer that drew my attention right back to the front of the classroom: "Baptism is a gift, and there are responsibilities that come with accepting the gift. But gifts are given in love, never by coercion. You have the choice to accept the gift or to refuse it. But each choice has its own implications. You sort of have to live into the gift to realize its blessing."

It had been three summers since I graduated from seminary, and I was working as a counselor in theology camp. Yes, theology camp. The room was full of fifty-seven high school kids. I listened transfixed as these young people tried to wrap their minds around the implications of their baptism and how it pertained to a faithful understanding of vocation. At their age I was duly intrigued by everything *but* my baptism. I was too interested in the surface of deep things, like the fairy-tale version of Buddhism I gleaned from underaged readings of books like Hermann Hesse's *Siddhartha*, and too enamored with Robert Smith from the British pop band *The Cure* to think of the "work of God."

As a teenager I had absolutely no sense that I had been given *any* kind

of gift, let alone one siphoned out of a tub of holy water. It took me a little longer than these kids to be re-membered into the church. I had asked Jesus into my heart because I had run out of options. I was seventeen years old, a freshman in college, sitting in a parked car outside the student center with Pastor Arnold from the local charismatic church and my charismatic-Lutheran (somewhat of an oxymoron, I know) junior counselor, Craig, who had knowingly gotten me into this mess in the first place. With no real idea what I was doing, I imagined myself with one foot in the door of salvation and the other dangling clumsily in everything I'd known until the past year. It was the start of what turned out to be an ongoing game of spiritual hokey pokey.

* * *

"Do you only listen to Christian music?" I asked my new holy friend, Melissa, as I flipped through her cassette tapes of Steven Curtis Chapman, Michael W. Smith, and Petra. It was sophomore year of college, and we were sitting in her dorm room making study notes for a class test. "Yeah, I had this huge purging session when I became a Christian and burned all my secular music." Her tone implied that I not only knew what she was talking about but clearly, considering that I had just recently let Jesus into my heart, I was on my way to stoke the bonfire myself, arms full of the deadly Bon Jovi and Bruce Springsteen. Needless to say, despite asking Jesus to share my heart with sophomore John Larson, the guy I was crushing on at the time, I never became the kind of Christian who burns music and I never fully believed that my relationship with God began in the parking lot that night. I think it started a longer time ago, before I could even spell the word *Christian* and before I could figure out whether or not I even wanted part of this thing.

My relationship with God began when I was four years old and went through a traumatic life changing experience. My sources tell me I was freed from sin, reborn as a child of God, made a member of Christ's body, grafted into the church and signed up as a staunch advocate of her mission. I remember it slightly differently—nonchalantly ambling my four-year-old way down the parish aisle, one hand in my mother's grasp, the other hand probably trailing pews all the way to the sinklike font. There I waited my turn as my newborn sister got sprinkled with water and mumbled over and parents and godparents smiled and hugged.

It is fascinating to me as a writer that the portal into the life of God is through water and word. Somehow the Holy Ghost shacks up in our souls with a verbal lease-to-buy agreement (depending on your tradition), and we are sealed to God for eternal life. I'm not going to pretend I get all that. But I do find the thought of it absolutely beautiful. Whenever I hear the words "You are sealed by the Holy Spirit in baptism and marked as Christ's own forever" during a baptismal service at church, I clutch my heart and gush as though I've just seen a baby panda rescued by a fleet of tiny forest nymph-like fairy angels. I find myself wanting to turn to my neighbor, my hand still over my heart, and whisper with tears in my eyes, "Did you see what just happened?" Sure, if I were to write out the entire liturgy for the baptismal rite, you would clearly see that it's not really about baby pandas and forest nymphs. It's actually more about being invited to die, perhaps to suffer in some respect, and most certainly to give up any notions you have of "happily ever after." But that's not really clever advertising, is it? These days I suspect you get more Christians with nymphs than you do with the grim reaper, hands down.

✳ ✳ ✳

I was sealed and rescued on September 10, 1977, a mild, uneventful autumn day in New York City. My parents took me to the font at Saint Nicholas of Tolentine's and in a strange sense, washed their hands of me and gave me back to God. I was born into the church smack-dab between Pentecost and Advent, destined to be Spirit-filled and curiously hungry, waiting for my life to passionately unfold like the dramatic liturgical seasons. Those nymphesque angels certainly changed this baby panda's life forever.

Reluctant Pilgrim

Some Christians don't believe in infant baptism (or toddler baptism in my case). In fact, when I recommitted my life to Christ as a college freshman, one friend desperately tried to convince me of my need for *re*baptism. She more or less implied that without being rebaptized I couldn't really expect to be drafted as a player for Team Jesus. But personally I'm glad I didn't have a real choice in the matter of my toddler baptism in the first place. If I had really known what I was getting myself baptized into, the life *and* the death of Christ, I'm not sure I could have signed the dotted line.

In the early centuries when the church was getting itself organized and rounding up more disciples for Christ, adult catechumens had to go through a three-year process before the Christian baptismal rite. It included teachings, examinations by congregational elders, fasting by the entire community, exorcisms, anointing, vigils, extensive prayers and worship, and eventually complete immersions, naked as the day is long, into a baptismal font that looked like a tomb. Some candidates were even turned away because they just didn't seem ready to embrace all the claims that baptism would make on their life—primarily that they now belonged first and fully to Christ. This meant a total albeit gradual transformation of their lives. I've always wondered how many folks today would actually agree to baptism if the stakes were still that high. Like I said it would have been a tough call for me. I'm not sure I could have agreed to "renounce all sinful desires that draw me from the love of God." That's a lot of stuff to give up when you think about it. (You might remember my thing for handbags.)

But then again, if I lived back in the first century, I probably could have done the adult baptism thing if my girlfriend Sophie did it with me. I have learned that I can do most things with a good girlfriend by my side. Sophie is one of my closest friends. We went to seminary together and then were lucky enough to work together the first couple of years out of school. We spent a lot of time in each other's offices, usually comparing notes on the latest Brad and Angelina headlines, which never seemed to get old for us.

Once in a while we talked theology. Chances are you would never guess we were seminary grads by our questions, answers and musings.

"Do you think you can lose your baptism?" I asked her one afternoon.

"What do you mean?"

"Like do you think the Holy Spirit can leave you?"

"Nazarenes believe you can lose your salvation. To me that's the same as losing the Holy Spirit."

Sophie is a recovering Nazarene currently serving time in the Episcopal Church.

"Hmm. Interesting. The Catholic Church says that baptism is an eternal seal. Once you're in, you ain't getting out."

"But don't you sort of have to live into your baptism? Like you can't just assume baptism is some kind of force field from sin can you?" she asked.

"No. I mean I guess not. But it's not like the Holy Spirit is going to get up and say 'Whoa, this dude is messed up. I'm outta here.' Anyway, don't Nazarenes believe that the Holy Spirit *is* kind of a sin force field? Like once you're baptized you're free from the grips of original sin?" (Maybe I was wrong. Maybe you can tell we went to seminary.)

"Yeah, Nazarenes do believe that technically, but I don't know how strictly it's interpreted," she said.

"The whole thing is kind of crazy really. I mean, think about it: it's almost nuts what we believe."

"I know," she replies, still typing away at the computer.

"The even crazier thing is that I never doubt it's true. I mean, I get shaky faith all the time and I wonder if God hears my prayers and if I'm praying for the wrong things and stuff like that, but I never doubt if the story is true."

"I know what you mean." She stops and looks back at me briefly, nodding her head in agreement.

"Oh, well," I say. "I forgot to tell you, I read that Jennifer Aniston is seeing some hot new British model guy. I really hope this works out for her."

Reluctant Pilgrim

* * *

Like I said, I went to seminary, and I know that there are many other ways to describe the rite of Christian baptism but I can't help wondering what the early versions of those fourth-century conversations sounded like. Saint Gregory of Nazianzus, that fourth-century Christian bishop of Constantinople, sat around with a couple of his buddies, two brothers named Basil the Great and Gregory of Nyssa (fourth-century Christian celebrities of sorts but feel free to refer to them by their spiritual mafia-esque nomenclature, the "Cappadocian Fathers") and revised what the church believes about the Trinity and the role of the Holy Spirit in humanity's salvation, otherwise known as the Nicene Creed. Coffee talk was a little different in those days.

Greg kind of got the point when he said, "Baptism is God's most beautiful and magnificent gift. . . . We call it gift, grace, anointing, enlightenment, garment of immortality, bath of rebirth, seal, and most precious gift. It is called *gift* because it is conferred on those who bring nothing of their own; *grace* since it is given even to the guilty; *Baptism* because sin is buried in the water; *anointing* for it is priestly and royal as are those who are anointed; *enlightenment* because it radiates light; *clothing* since it veils our shame; *bath* because it washes; and *seal* as it is our guard and the sign of God's Lordship." Exactly what I was thinking, but I wanted to give Saint Gregory his props.

Anyway, back to my baptism in the Catholic Church, I just assumed I could get at God if given the right opportunity. For starters, I thought God was a he. Don't ask me to analyze why, it's just what I thought, and it worked out fine for me for the most part. For more starters, I thought he lived at Saint Nick's in the back rooms of the sacristy and he only took visitors once a week. I imagined God sort of reclining God's amorphous self in the sacristy behind the altar watching somewhat disaffectedly as people filed into the pews, and making obligatory notes on who showed up and who didn't, disinterested in who actually came because really, if we didn't show up to worship him, it was our loss, not his. I was kind of in awe of that God, the way Richie beheld the Fonz on *Happy Days*, eager, pretty much on the inner circle but instinctively sensing there was a limit to how close I could get. Then there was Jesus, who rumor had it was both God *and* God's Son, a little trickier to wrap my six-year-old mind around. I know it's hard to believe but I hadn't quite figured out the whole Trinity thing yet (umm, and I'm still working on it).

But there was Jesus in plain view every Sunday, thirty feet above me, suspended in the air on a humongous cross, head hung dejectedly to his chest, feet and hands nailed in bronze. I sensed Jesus was pretty important, because he was God's Son and somehow related to me and the other strangers in the church. Jesus died. That much was clear. After that, the facts—the story—got murky for me. But that was the story I bought: God was the most important, Jesus came next, and he was related to God and somehow to me. From the number of people that showed up every week I had to think that church was a necessary part of life, even with the special men in quirky dresses.

Each Sunday I secretly hoped that God would come out from the back and surprise us, catching everyone in the middle of eating and drinking "the body and blood of Christ." I won't even try and explain how weird that part was for me. I really believed people were eating real flesh and drinking real blood. And because only the adults did it, I imagined it was serious business and you had to be prepared in some special way for that kind of thing. Yet, honestly, in that context of already bizarre rituals, although it seemed a very strange thing to do, it also seemed okay. I was never scared of the idea of it, more just awed with childish disbelief. As for getting at God, I remember distinctly feeling on edge, curiously anxious at the thin line of separation between me and God, that single door to the left of the altar. I would stand up, leaning my small six-year-old frame over the pew in front of me and strain my neck, hoping to steal a glimpse of God between the swishing robes of altar boys passing back and forth through that door. It was obviously up to me to catch him because something made me believe that God took up too much space and was too overwhelming a presence to enter the sanctuary where I sat with my family. So he had

a spokesman, the priest, and that was fine. But still, I used to daydream during Mass about making a mad dash from the pews before my mother could stop me and hightailing it through that back door on the heels of an altar boy. Then I would see God and I would be satisfied. I don't think I have ever stopped calculating mad dashes to catch glimpses of God.

Chapter 5

Eternal God,
it might take me an eternity to know you.
Thank you that time is of little
consequence to you.

In the Roman Catholic rite by which I was baptized, Christian initiation happens in threes: baptism, confirmation, and Eucharist. I was baptized before I'd reached "the age of reason," before I could confirm that I did in fact sort of understand what was being asked of me as I renounced Satan and took up Christ, before I could ask questions of what exactly my responsibilities would be as a member of the universal church and my local parish. Baptism was free, no charge for divine grace, no merit needed on my part. One, two three, in the name of the Father, Son, and Holy Ghost, my original sin inherited from my distance relatives Adam and Eve, and my personal sin, which was probably quite a bit seeing that I was already four years old, was wiped out and I was sealed to God *forever*. I could argue over how or why this happens, pontificate over the mystery of it all, but why? It sounds like I got a pretty good deal and I'm taking it. However, that was only Stage 1. Stage 2, confirmation, apparently would further bless me with the gift of God's grace, the gifts of the Holy Ghost, and a deeper awareness of my place in the church and her mission. And this is where my problem began.

Three years after I was baptized, my family picked up and moved to another country. I was seven years old when we left New York and went to Nigeria. In the shuffle of luggage and new addresses and shifting time zones, I skipped childhood catechesis, that Catholic ritual of teaching children what it means to be baptized into Christ and into the life of the church. After catechesis, children go through the rite of Confirmation

when they acknowledge having gained some understanding of their baptism and agree to try and live into it. One could argue, I guess, that I'm half-graced. I never got confirmed in the Catholic Church or in any church for that matter. I never got the chance to say yes or no to active duty. I never sat through Confirmation classes where teachers explained the faith to me or gave me some inkling about what it meant to be a so-called "new creation," what it meant for my identity both in and out of the church. No one ever told me that church community was important, that crossing the threshold into new life with God had anything to do with anyone else but me. In my interpretation, I was still the center of the universe. Even if it was God's.

But the Spirit caught hold of me anyway, because when we moved to West Africa, I didn't forget the sanctuaries close to home or the bowls of holy water in church entryways. I didn't forget what I'd inferred about Jesus through the small gestures, the kneeling and body crossing, the colorful stained glass, the statues of Mary, the singing, the processions, the reading of words I recognized without understanding their significance. In my young mind, the church was a type of carnival, and I at least understood on some level that when I took part of that strange water ritual, I was grafted onto the growing body of people who played out their lives in this holy drama of mourning and celebration. I could tell just from the symbols and rituals that death and life were constantly at play with one another, and somehow those little pools of water placed at distinct points around the church were life sources, where you reaffirmed again and again that your life was bound up in Christ and your story began with God and ended with God. And then, without grasping the implications of hope and danger, I fell in love with God somewhere between my baptism at age four in a little Queens neighborhood parish in New York City and the age of seven when I first spotted those merchants outside the cathedral gates in Lagos, Nigeria.

The church says that humans are by nature religious beings, so maybe I shouldn't be surprised that after missing my own confirmation I instinctively just started groping after God. A baptized Christian without operating instructions can only be left to her own devices. What I learned about the faith I picked up from being keenly observant, annoyingly curious, and, quite frankly, pretty weird. When I should have been learning about creeds, sacraments, and prayer, or at least collecting dolls, I was instead collecting tiny, pendant-sized crucifixes and displaying them in glass cases hidden in drawers. Somewhere along the way I began to believe that if the holy water in the narthex font touched my mouth and I swallowed some by mistake, I would be transformed into a free-floating ethereal being. Yes, that was me by the age of seven—a God-loving, crucifix-hoarding, four-eyed kid both cognizant and fearful of the power of holy water and the presence of the Spirit. Clearly, by all cultural standards, I was on the path to being the most popular girl in school.

So there you have it—I've been keeping Jesus in boxes since the second grade. At first I treasured the Son of God in my little red-and-white Hello Kitty jewelry box. After three years of living in Nigeria, my mother, my little sister, and I left my dad and moved to the Ivory Coast. Later, I thought it was a good idea to move Jesus from the Hello Kitty sanctuary to a little plastic box the size of half of my thumb with a clear, see-through lid. I used to keep a little iridescent blue fishbowl pebble in it that Chrissy Madesen gave me during the fifth grade. At best, religion—because that's all it was at the time—was interesting, the way an only child too wrapped up in her own imagination begins to play mad scientist with tiny figurines of the Christ child, the crucified Christ, and the Virgin Mary. Gently turning these minute religious artifacts over with an index finger, feigning a vaguely Eastern European accent, and whispering, "Aha, veery, veery interesting." That's basically how I approached the church, somewhat lost in the reverence of word and sacrament and holy gestures but even more so in the curious behavior of the natives and the decorative elements of their spiritual habitat: the kneeling, the standing, the light snack in the middle of service, all "veery veery interesting." Then in a moment of transcendental enlightenment, I opened the box and sprinkled shiny red heart-shaped confetti at the bottom of the cross—the kind of confetti love you get at greeting card stores. I thought the red hearts were a brilliantly

imaginative move, divine creativity at its best—Jesus and the hearts of the world and the stuff about his blood—which I didn't really get, but I knew the red hearts were brilliant. Once in a while I would bring Jesus out to look at him and to remind myself that I loved him—what I could remember about him—and, odd as it may seem, I started to believe that little 14k-gold crucified Jesus loved me back.

* * *

If I haven't made it clear yet, I take the idea of baptism pretty seriously. I don't fully understand it, but that itself seems to make sense to me, that it would be a little difficult to wrap my mind around a sacrament, a means by which somehow God continually reveals God's self to humanity. There has to be some inexplicable mystery running through the currents and canals of God's grace. What I do understand is that once I have joined the crowd of carnival goers, I am invited to put on these new metaphysical outfits, these clothes of eternal life, if you will, that help me identify myself as part of the unfolding drama. Maybe baptism is the first step because besides grafting me into new life, it is also when, knowingly or not, I put on the death mask of Christ.

Maybe it should be no surprise that I have struggled to embrace the full implications of this initial ritual, the call to a certain way of daily living, of practicing new life amongst strangers while enacting little personal deaths—some private, some very public—all supposedly grounded in love. Wherever I find another Christian I apparently find another brother and sister, and my growing community is supposed to help me live out those little deaths because we're all in it together. In the grand scheme of things, my little deaths affect you. But it doesn't always work out that way. I didn't walk away from the font that eventful day bug-eyed with awe and gratitude over my newfound family members, eager to let them help me die a thousand little deaths.

Instead, I spent the next thirty years stumbling my way through the church, bumping into teachings and teachers I couldn't fully understand or want to understand, rearranging my place as confusion, longing, and hope permitted. After my parents' split and going to live with my mom, our part of the family left the Catholic Church, nothing dramatic and purgatory-inducing really; we just moved a few countries away to the Ivory Coast and sort of didn't go back to Mass. I tiptoed in and out of almost every mainline denomination you can think of. People find it somewhat amazing when I tell them that I have spent time attending Anglican, Charismatic, Methodist, Catholic, Presbyterian, Lutheran, and Free Covenant churches. They wonder how I can have any sense of Christian identity if my faith has been doled out to so many denominations. I don't know. I still struggle with Christian identity, but I imagine and hope that it has more to do with the struggle to fully live into the life Christ calls me to than being confused because I've shared the bread and the cup with Christians by various names.

I consider myself gifted to have worshiped amongst so many church communities and to be a part of the different ways the Spirit moves amongst us. I believe in demon possession as much as I believe that the bread and the wine actually turn into the body and blood of Christ. I think Jonah could indeed have been swallowed by one of Moby Dick's ancestors, but I'm not sure that's the entire point of the story. God could throw a man in the belly of a whale and rescue him alive three days later, but the more miraculous thing to me is that God offers not only forgiveness and redemption but a way for us to crawl out from our own tendencies to live in the underbelly of life. And I believe that being a part of the church means giving up a sense of ownership of anything and any sense of individual rights, because ultimately it's about love of the other and taking on the servant posture of a crucified Christ. Though there's that minor detail of how we can't really love "the other" until we learn to love ourselves in a way that mirrors the reality of being made in the image of God. It's scary and definitely not easy. But that's what Christ asks us to do.

Even with my struggle, there is a lot of grace in being part of the church. God doesn't expect us to get it correct right away. There's room for messing up and scribbling outside the lines, for throwing temper tantrums

and stubbornly refusing to do as we're told. God is patient in ways we'll never fathom. There's also room for growth. Even though we are a part of the community, we are more sustained by the community than feeding it. I used to guilt trip myself about the feeling that I didn't have anything to give to the church, sneaking in a little late, and sliding into a back pew where I would drink in everything I could from sermons and prayers and holy Communion. Then I would slip back out like a thief in the night somewhat able to make it through another week. I didn't want to talk to anyone or join Bible studies or commit to Sunday school. I wanted to come in and fill up my empty tank without bumping into other customers. I don't feel too guilty about such things anymore because I think those are valid stages of spiritual growth, being greedily hungry for God and consumed with feeding your insatiable hunger, like that man-eating plant in *Little Shop of Horrors*.

Maybe I don't feel guilty because I live under the assumption that God is always at work in our lives even before we know it. I think that's what grace is, that God is sort of stalking us and preparing us in small yet significant ways for the shock of becoming church and trying to live into the absurdity of church. Really it's not normal. We do not naturally group ourselves with strangers who are different from us in so many visible and not so visible ways. We do not readily give up the things we want in order to provide for people we don't know or even necessarily like. We do not give our time, resources, and privacy to just anyone. But that's what church calls us to do and that's why I have such a hard time with it, Protestant or Catholic. And as you've noticed, I've tried both.

Chapter 6

Crucified Christ,
you know of the agony of death and yet you call
us to die to self, to the things that keep us from
you, and to the past that shadows the light of a
transformed future.

I forget that you have this way
of dying over and over again
And hitting me with the news
in the middle of blue days
and moods and coffeeshops
And all I can do is sit until
the news dissipates and
no longer seems like news
for the moment.

Just before my thirtieth birthday, my father died unexpectedly and I lost the ability to pray.

I wish I could put my hands on it, on how I felt after the phone call, on walking outside into the January winter air and finding my way to my girlfriend Lisa's car, and sitting in the passenger seat, and hearing her voice, and not knowing what she was saying or what I was supposed to say or why people outside were still walking around as though nothing had happened. I wish I could put my finger right on what I felt as I unlocked my front door and went inside only to have to come back out again because the air inside was too thick, and sitting on my front steps as my neighbor walked by, not knowing what to say to anyone. As I processed the news, the God I had clung to so desperately all these years seemed to disappear slowly and suddenly all at once. I couldn't find God anywhere—not on

my knees, not in the peace of sleep, and not in my journal musings. He was gone and I felt like I was hyperventilating in the dark.

I hadn't seen my father in eleven years until I saw him at his funeral. In all those years since my parents' divorce, I had gone back to Nigeria maybe half a dozen times. It was kind of like I left my father, my country, and the Catholic Church all at once. Whoever I was changed in the space of a ten-hour plane ride away from the place markers of my early childhood. So after an absence of eleven years, I returned to Nigeria to bury my father, down a red clay dirt road to the village of my paternal ancestors—a village I had only been to once when I was six. The memory of making that trip for the funeral is still clear to me.

* * *

I couldn't remember the last time I was in this southern part of the country. The small, crowded local airport in Enugu was filled with haggard women whose overused bodies had aged beyond their years. Their sagging breasts and folds of skin around their middles suggested a life too busy to trouble with exterior appearances. Restless children clung clumsily to their calves, draping small arms wherever they could get a hold amidst the large plastic bins and containers filled with market treasures. Skinny weightless men in dampened short-sleeve cotton shirts and wrinkled trousers stood through the heat and weak air conditioning. I remember sitting as neatly and compactly as possible—trying to creatively shrink my sweaty body so as not to touch anything with my skin, besides the seat I was on. I held my hand luggage close on my lap, grateful not to have to worry about numerous bags on the dirty tiled floor. Scrunched up inside myself, I waited impatiently for the rest of my luggage. I was crabby and tired after getting off the cramped, stuffy, suffocating, sweat-scented plane that brought me here to see my father for probably the last time. I couldn't imagine making future long treks back to visit his grave site.

I know I stuck out like a sore thumb, like a spoiled American African who seemed uncomfortable amongst her own people. I was shamefully aware of being a stranger in my own country. I was the one educated abroad who returned home to wrinkle my nose at the places and people I used to navigate in and amongst as a small child. I was the one who couldn't write a memoir about having lived through the trials and sufferings of Africa. I knew so little of Africa as it was; all my knowledge seemed full of touristy flashbacks and colonized thought patterns. *Oyebo*—"white man"—is what my aunts and uncles called me—the term usually reserved for white Westerners or those Africans who "forgot" they were African. It was always said with a smile and a shaking of the head. It wasn't that I'd forgotten I was African—I just never fully learned what that meant. I pieced my knowledge together once I was back overseas, through the questions people asked me, the comments people made, the quizzical looks on faces when I said my name aloud. I discovered in bits and pieces what it meant to be African from the constant sense of being lost or misplaced, out of place in Oxford, England; Wales; Henley on Thames; Northfield, Minnesota; Somerville, Massachusetts; Chicago, Illinois; Seattle, Washington; Bozeman, Montana; and many other places. I piece together parts of my country the same way I piece together memories of my father.

* * *

I've worked it out in my mind that the last time I talked to my Dad was at his funeral where I kept turning toward the gate expecting to see him run in late, apologizing for not being able to join us sooner. I knew that when he came, he would sit beside me, in the seat I'd saved for him, take my hand and link our fingers securely together the way he used to when I was six or seven. He'd give me a quick, reassuring smile before directing his attention to the somber event before us.

"That looks nothing like me, Chi" (that's what he called me) is the first thing he would say, and I would have to agree. The shriveled, powdered face in the casket looked like it was made of Formica, and it wasn't really my father. Here he was beside me. I could tell you what he'd had for breakfast, an orange and two boiled eggs with toast, like always. That's

what he used to have when we were kids living with him, when we were all a family. I acquired my taste for tea when I was in the second grade—a china cup and saucer with a steeping bag of Lipton tea, a few large drops of Carnation condensed milk, and two sugar cubes. Growing up in Lagos we had tea every morning, a bowl of Kellogg cornflakes or Rice Krispies, and sometimes a croissant. My father was a creature of habit who didn't like change. He still had the olive green 1979 200SLC Mercedes-Benz that carried me to and from second, third, and fourth grade in the early eighties. A few days ago we saw it parked in the garage at his house, our old house, back in Lagos. His tenants hadn't heard of his death.

Anyway, after breakfast, I am sure that on his way to his bedroom to get dressed for the day, for his funeral, he had hummed that same riff I had heard since I was seven, "la di di da . . ." And now here he was, late as always, just like when he used to pick us up from school. But even then I had worked out acceptable excuses for all his actions.

"Chi, who selected that coffin?"

"Mom did. She did practically everything. We went to Mr. Adewalo's shop in Lagos on Johnson Street and ordered it for you. She kept saying that she wanted you to have the best casket, simple but classy looking. She even had that cross put on the lid. I was there with her and Emeka and Aunty Tobs. It felt so weird, Dad, being there, in that shop in Lagos. The owner was the same man who had helped mom get the casket for her brother, Uncle Tom, when he died all those years back."

Now he was quiet and I couldn't read him. He turned away from me to look at my mother and there was water in his eyes. It was a rare thing to see my father tear up. Mom wouldn't look at him though. I didn't know if she could see him, but I didn't want to call attention to us just yet. I needed him to myself for a little longer.

"What's wrong, Dad?"

"Your mum did all that for me?" His voice was quiet, disbelieving but not surprised.

"Mom paid for practically everything, Dad. You're not surprised, are you? You know that's how she is. She even got you the Mercedes ambulance. She wanted

to get you a new black one, but by the time she got to Enugu they had all been booked."

"Why didn't your Uncle Michael or Aunt Janette reserve one on time?"

"You're asking me? Since Mom got here, your brothers and sisters have hardly done anything. They haven't seen her in twenty years, and all of a sudden they can't even organize your funeral. I'm sorry, Dad, but it's been something else. After all you've done for them. It makes me so angry. I've barely been able to look at them this whole week! At the mortuary, Janette just stood around looking so incompetent and . . .

"Chi, calm down my dear, they've . . ."

"Why should I calm down? Did you see Joseph's right hand? He's wearing your ring! You know your gold ring you've had for over thirty years. And you're not even in the ground. Can you believe the audacity?"

He's silent again. I wonder if I've said too much. I want to keep him talking, here next to me. His silence reminds me of that person in the coffin. I am not ready for more silences. I fumble words out of my mouth, to hold him, to hold me a little longer.

"Dad, I'm sorry. I know this is the last thing you want to hear today. I just get so angry. And look how they're all staring at us, like they can't believe we're your children. They don't have anything to tell us? They just smile at us like we're stupid two-year-olds who can't understand what's going on. Nobody's even offered to tell us about you, Dad."

And suddenly I'm twelve years old again, sitting on his lap, proud and toughened, trying not to cry when he asks me how I'd feel if he got married again.

"It's all right, my dear. Don't worry. Everything will be all right. I know this is hard for you. It's okay, you hear?" He squeezes my hand and it feels warm and familiar but longing sits in my stomach, more at home than anything else. I have to stop myself from letting that first tear fall. If I start crying I know I won't be able to stop.

"Tell me, Dad."

"Tell you what, my dear?"

"About you, the stairs, that morning, the hospital all those months, the

*feeling leaving your legs, getting our phone calls, talking to Mom, the coma . . .
tell me, Dad."*

"Chi, come now, we are right in the middle of this thing, you people have to
go and walk around the coffin before they move it to the grave site. My dear, don't
worry. It's okay, you hear."

It was so typical of him to deflect emotions, any emotions—mine or
his. I let him get away with it for all those years, but I couldn't stop now.
This felt like my last chance. So I just plowed on, telling him all I knew,
admitting I wasn't completely in the dark, a child who doesn't know what
goes on between grown ups, between parents or siblings.

"Peter said you just collapsed at the top of the stairs one morning and from
then on you couldn't walk. You had no feelings from the waist down. He said you
had been in the hospital since October. That was four months ago. He said nobody
would tell him how serious it was. That's why he didn't tell us for a whole month.
But Janette knew. Theresa knew. They took care of you in the hospital everyday.
Why didn't your sisters tell Peter or Joseph? They are your brothers! Why didn't
anyone tell us?"

* * *

It was like time to lower the coffin into the grave. Dad doesn't want to
look. He stands to the side and gently pushes me forward when it's time
to throw the fistful of dirt. I want to jump in the grave, unable to process
the finality, Dad here in a corner of a small village down a dusty red clay
dirt road sixty miles from the town of Enugu, a plane ride from Lagos, a
long journey back to Europe and then to America, back to the South, to
North Carolina on my short street in the middle of Durham. In flashes,
the distance between him and me engulfs me. I still long for him in a way
that is as subtle as breathing. Sometimes I forget I am doing it, but I do not
know how to live without it.

Chapter 7

Incarnate God,
you are the first Word of all words. Help me find
ways to articulate my love for you when my words
escape me.

When I got back from the funeral to my home in Durham, I couldn't find my prayers for months, but I still ached for God. It just got even harder to access God. I found myself drawn to numbly reading the Anglican Book of Common Prayer, hoping that it really was true what I had heard, that liturgy tried and tested through the centuries can help sustain the weak and the weary by the mere habit of practice. I chose to believe that when I repeated those old prayers, somehow God would receive them as my very own. And because I didn't know where else to go, I tried to wiggle my way back into Mass to see if things still fit like they used to when I was child.

* * *

"I've been thinking about going back to Mass." I say it casually, running my index finger across book bindings and feigning interest in Mystics on a top shelf of the small campus bookstore. My friend Jessica, the store manager, looks unperturbed, completely missing the leap I'd just made.

"Are you still going to Our Lady of the Cross?" I ask.

"Yeah, but lately I've been out of town for dance shows." Jessica is barely over five feet, a tiny pixieish thirty-five-year-old woman who hardly looks her age. She's a devout Catholic with a penchant for belly dancing and body piercing—a safe choice to help me fidget my way back into Mass.

Reluctant Pilgrim

"Are you going this weekend?" I ask.

"I'm planning on it. You should come with me."

"That'd be great," I say.

"I go to the 7:45 AM service 'cause it's less crowded and it's shorter." Already I know this is good.

"Okay. Should I just swing by and pick you up?"

"I can come get you," she replies. "I usually roll out of bed at 7:30, throw on some jeans, and head out. It's Catholic—we don't dress up for each other." She laughs and throws her hand out in the air, like someone confident and secure in a home church. For the rest of the week I catch myself nervously anticipating the coming Sunday.

* * *

I'm on my front porch steps trying to finish my coffee before Jessica's white Honda turns the corner of my street. I'm wondering if I'm overdressed in my ankle-length blue skirt and the black lace shawl over my shoulders. I've chosen a fitted black tee shirt to downplay the outfit. I want to look casual, to play it cool; but it had taken me thirty minutes to decide what to wear this morning. I felt I should look nice for this first time back. I sit on my steps as anxiety, nervousness, and excitement volley back and forth in my stomach. I am grateful to be going with Jessica. I figure the liturgy will seem less intimidating if I'm sitting beside a seasoned Catholic friend. It had taken losing my father for me to gather up the courage to go back. I had thought about it before, felt compelled even but stayed resistant— too many unknowns and irrational fears about what could happen once I got to Mass. How would I genuflect, when would I genuflect? I'd only recently found out that my childhood practice of kneeling to the ground even had a name. I worried about whether or not I would receive the Eucharist, whether I was allowed to go up or not, how I felt about being excluded from eating the body of Christ. I worried about what it would feel like to be left standing in the pews when everyone else, including Jessica, walked by me to receive. I wondered if people would be able to tell that I hadn't been to Mass in twenty-two years. I wondered how long it would take me to stop feeling like a trespasser.

We get to the church a few minutes early just as I had hoped. Now we could walk into the sanctuary unnoticed and I could pick a pew in the back from which to worship and observe.

"Where do you want to sit?" Jessica asks.

I do a quick survey of the people in the back pews—young white family, middle-aged Latino couple, pious-looking old woman with a white shawl over her hair. "Let's sit over there, next to that woman with the shawl."

We sit down and I begin my familiar routine of trying to get a feel for this new worship space. This was how I got used to a place, to sanctuaries, sitting inconspicuous in back pews until I felt safe enough, surveying the land. Jessica turns to face me with her copy of *Gatherings*, the book of worship, opened it to the right page and says, "This is the liturgy we use."

"Thanks."

* * *

By my third visit to Mass, I noticed that the Eucharist was the center of the service. Everything seemed to lead up to that time of feasting on the Body of God. Even the homily seemed circumstantial, one more hoop to get through before the Celebration. Recognizing this made me feel even more of an outsider, an observer needing to relearn my way back to the table. I was an expat trying to make my way home again. But I had been away since childhood, and now, returning as an adult, I noticed certain customs for the first time, ways of contorting oneself into the crevices of this holy space that spoke of mystery and ritual: people bowing and genuflecting before sitting in their pews; lectors and celebrants genuflecting before the altar before stepping onto holy ground; everyone remaining standing until all had received and returned to the pews, as though in reverence for simply being in the presence of the body of Christ. And the haunting words "Lord, I am not worthy to receive you but only speak the

word and I shall be healed." The first time I heard these words, I found myself repeating them over and over in my head, marveling at the humility of such words.

I went back to Mass off and on again for the next six months, trying different parishes, waiting to see if anyone noticed I'd visited, and then leaving and coming back again. I wanted a priest to say to me, "Oh, we hoped you'd be back. Let's make sure we set a time to chat over tea before you disappear again." I wanted someone in my pew to read my mind and reach over and say, "Oh, don't worry, half of us here are lapsed Catholics. We just had kids and decided it was time to come back. Welcome home!" I wanted to feel like I *was* coming back home after a long journey away. I wanted these strangers to feel like family because we were all Catholic, and being Catholic meant universal family right? *Wrong!* All I ended up feeling was like I'd walked into a private club where people had been members for generations and everyone was related to everyone else and no one had time to offer the visitor an application for membership because really, if you need an application, surely you're not at home.

* * *

I couldn't figure out if the tugging I felt toward the Catholic Church was nostalgia for my childhood and what I knew of my father or really a desire to claim my Catholic identity because that's where I imagined I might find the community I was looking for, because I imagined I might receive the gushing, unquestioning welcome of a prodigal daughter. Whatever it was, it felt like starting all over again in a strange way that I was intrigued by but not fully comfortable with. Each Mass I attended seemed to provoke memories of being a child in the church and the awe and love of God that sprinkled my early years in the church. And mixed in were memories of my father, home in Nigeria, the longest memories I have of being rooted and connected to a place, a people, and a family. The first ten years of my life were spent in the Catholic Church, the time when my parents were still together, when all my siblings and I lived in the same house, and my days' routine was set solidly in family life. It was a time when I could dance and dodge around a crucified Christ with the playful passion of a smitten, mystified, and rooted child.

* * *

After close to seven months of Mass hopping, I left as easily as I had come. My time as an expat in the Protestant church seemed to have made it too difficult to come back home. And the aftershock of realizing that my child-hood home was really behind me drained any desire or motivation to go to church at all. I gave myself permission take a bitter sabbatical from worship.

Taking a sabbatical from church turned out to be fairly easy at first. I quickly got used to having Sunday mornings to myself again, irritably tossing away guilt like an unnecessary pillow keeping me from a good night's sleep. With a bit of an attitude I told God I hoped he was big enough to take my leave of absence from church because I just couldn't muster up the energy to walk back into any of the congregations where I'd sat on the fringes the past few years. It felt a little like the sadness you feel after you finally decide to stop trying to make a bad relationship work— defeated resignation tinged with stabs of relief and momentary freedom. Only in this case, I didn't feel like I was giving up on God, just on the idea of church and loving Christian churchy community. Sure, it occurred to me that maybe I was part of the problem in this stagnant church relation-ship I was pulling out of, but it's hard to work on your end of a relation-ship when the other end doesn't even think there is a problem.

Besides, let's face it. There's a lot of convenience and comfort to hav-ing a personal God. I get to pray about what I want, when I want and with whom I want. Sure, I feel guilty when I don't pray for people in develop-ing countries on a regular basis or when I forget to ask God to illumine the minds of world leaders to strive for peace. But it's so much more interest-ing to pray for the things in my line of vision, the various sundry garden-variety worries that plague me and the people around me, like if I'll ever

run into that really attractive guy who happens to be into God but not in the scary "Want to drink the Kool-Aid" kind of way. I hate admitting that, but the truth is I am a pretty selfish person, which makes trying to be a community-focused Christian very challenging—the biggest challenge being to understand that there is no other actual type of Christian.

Part of the problem is that part of me fears what really being involved with the church will demand of me. And I'm not even talking about the peer pressure to join church committees and pretend that there is nothing else I'd rather be doing than planning retreats and teaching Sunday school. I'm talking about the other stuff: the learning to be a disciple; the "taking up your cross" clause; the "working out your salvation in fear and trembling" small print; the "doing even greater works than me" ditty. When I think about all that, I get overwhelmed.

I know that part of committing to a church and its people means entering spaces where others have a right to get to know me. This flies right in the face of my screwed-up sense of self. It also means having to submit to a God I did not design, a God I sometimes find hard to relate to.

Chapter 8

When you died that way
so up and all of a sudden
in the middle of my musings
of coming back to you
God left me too
So up and all of a sudden
with strange voices I didn't know
and midnight wrestling matches
over proving my love
If I loved him
I would go back
to give myself completely
If I loved him
better than I had loved you
I would not be afraid of confrontation
and the death of dreams
of a reconciled Father.

"Can I tell you a secret?" my voice was weary as I asked my girlfriend Anna.

"Sure, Honey."

"I think God wants me to be a nun." I laid it out with the deep resignation I felt in my heart. Anna looked at me with the concerned shock I considered duly appropriate.

"Honey, what do you mean? Why do you say that?"

Anna has a doctorate in Christian ethics and teaches at a fancy private university where the undergrad girls dress as though every day is an open casting call for *Sex and the City*. Anna likes to challenge her students to give up shopping and watching TV for the semester they take her class. Then she invites them to community meetings for living wages and support of illegal immigrants. She loves Jane Austen, substituting carob chips for chocolate, and taking her eight-year-old daughter to protest rallies against the death penalty whenever possible. She can be deeply sympathetic and brutally honest.

"Because," I said, almost on the verge of tears, "I don't want to go to Mass anymore and since I want to be married I'm almost sure God must think I want a husband more than I want God and so he's going to make me become a nun to prove how much I really do love him." It sounded more logical in my head, but I hoped Anna's PhD status would help her grasp the obvious connections I was trying to make.

"OK, back up, Sweetie. First of all, forget the whole 'not wanting to go to Mass' thing for now. God can handle that. I'm more worried that you think God makes us prove our love for him by 'punishing' us into the cloister. Where did *that* come from?"

All I could do was weep at her question. I was crying for all sorts of unrelated things—my dad's death, my singleness, my fatigue with deal-ing with life on my own, and my growing inability to find a church where I felt safe and seen and sewn into the fabric of congregational life. I told her how I wasn't sleeping well and how I woke up in the middle of the night panicked that God wanted me to be a nun and it made me feel like I couldn't breathe. It got to the point that I was afraid of the dark, and of going to bed.

"Honey, I think you should consider the possibility that the voices you're hearing are not of God."

"What do you mean?" I sniffled.

"Well, God may be calling you to singleness, but I don't think he'd call you this way. And I think, if anything, God would want you to deal with the death of your father, to really mourn and process that before he asked you to take a vow of celibacy and join the sisterhood."

"I don't see your point," I sniffled some more.

"Sweetheart, God is a God of order, not chaos. I just can't imagine God would burden you with such chaotic fear about singleness and convents when it seems the most healing thing you could do for yourself right now is attend to the major loss you've recently experienced. There is nothing healthy or healing about what you're describing to me."

I didn't say anything, but I could feel the light flow of hope and relief wash over me. Anna suggested I think about seeing a spiritual director she knew, Sister Catherine. "Great," I thought, "she wants me to see a nun and then God will probably confirm my call and I won't be able to do it and God will think I don't love him when really I love God to pieces. I just want the chance to love God with a hunk by my side. A kind, generous, peace-seeking, baby-loving hunk."

"Okay," I sobbed.

✳ ✳ ✳

Sister Catherine told me that if God was calling me to be a nun, chances were I would be excited about it and not react to the mere thought as if someone was putting a pillow over my face and suffocating me to death. That made sense in her office. I knew I would like Sister Catherine as soon as I met her, even if I didn't have any idea what a spiritual director was. It took me a few weeks to call her, but as soon as I walked into her office I felt a sense of safety and calm that I hadn't experienced in a long time. The room was divided by a tall bookcase separating her massage table from her "directing" corner. She explained that the table was for clients who felt comfortable and interested in body work as part of their spiritual direction. The section where we would meet had a large window overlooking a green pasture. There were two comfortable chairs, a table with a candle and a box of Kleenex on it, and a framed poster of the Appian Way, ancient Rome's oldest surviving road, on the wall. As she guided

me to sit down, I stole quick glances at her bookshelves, wondering what I'd gotten myself into. I was able to catch sight of only one or two titles, *Praying Our Goodbyes*, by Joyce Rupp, and *The Road to Daybreak*, by Henri Nouwen. I knew enough about those two Catholic writers and spiritual mentors from personal readings to make me more relaxed. When we sat down, Sister Catherine asked if she could begin with a prayer to invite the holy into our midst and to keep us open to God's wisdom and presence.

"Sure," I said.

After the prayer my first session began. I stared at the picture of the Appian Way as though I'd never seen a cobbled road before.

"So why don't you tell me a little bit about yourself." She was trying to ease me into it.

"My dad died six months ago, but I think God is calling me to be a nun, and Anna suggested I talk to you." I went straight for the throat.

"Okay."

Pause.

"Can you tell me more about your father's death?" She asked gently.

I told her that my father had lived in Nigeria and we hadn't spoken in years but that I'd always put off really reconnecting with him until I had more time but then he had died suddenly of prostate cancer and that we'd only found out he was sick two weeks before he died and that I was planning to take some time off after I finished seminary to go visit with him but that he died without us even knowing how seriously ill he was. Then I took a breath. I told her how a year ago he had tried reconnecting with me for months but I never took his phone calls because I just wasn't ready to deal with all the questions and hurt I still had from the separation decades ago and how he'd childishly handled it, choosing to punish my mom for leaving him by cutting us off financially and selfishly letting us kids bear the brunt of it. I told her how much I still loved him and how strange it was to go back for the funeral and to bury him. And then I stopped talking and started weeping.

Sister Catherine let me cry and handed me some Kleenex. When I pulled myself together, she said quietly, "Maybe we should put the nun thing aside for now."

* * *

Later that afternoon after a much-needed nap, I got on my knees and prayed and cried to God, asking him to allow me to experience him as a loving and merciful and comforting presence in my life. I prayed that he would help me fight one battle at a time and that he would take away all those overbearing and suffocating thoughts. I prayed to be open to whatever he called me to but asked first that he would help me mourn the death and absence of my father. And while on my knees, I remembered what Anna had said about not every voice being from God, so I prayed, for safe measure, that any voice that wasn't from God would be cast out in the name of Jesus. And I told God I needed space to rest, to stop worrying about my religious life, to stop feeling guilty or frustrated about whether or not I could find a church, and to stop conjuring up new sacrifices God must want me to offer. I prayed to learn to find myself again in daily mundane rhythms of life, to slowly relearn how to embrace God's grace. I told God that even though I couldn't seem to find him in church right now, I was hoping to find him in the voices and company of my friends and family, and in my time with Sister Catherine. I was going to rely on their discernment and wisdom for me for a while because I didn't have the energy to figure things out on my own. My worship and liturgy would instead look like mustering the energy to go for walks, to cook healthy meals and eat on my front porch with friends, to read mindless fiction, to repeat the words of the Daily Office and claim them as my own heartfelt prayers.

* * *

I started seeing Sister Catherine once a week, and within two months I experienced what seemed like a spiritual transformation in which I was radically broken open and the thick outer shell I had maintained for so long was cracking; pieces were falling off one by one, slowly and painfully. And I learned the difference between a *therapist* and a *spiritual director*. Sister Catherine helped me think through my relationship with God

and how different areas of my life affected or were seemingly affected by my sense of spiritual self.

"I know this season of the church year is called Ordinary Time because it's not a special season like Advent or Lent, and the weeks are simply numbered, but I like to think of it meaning plain and uneventful time more so than ordinal," I told Sister Catherine during one session.

"Why?" she asked.

"Because it kind of feels like a gift to me, to be trying to experience God in really simple ways during the church season of Ordinary Time when nothing exciting is happening like Easter or Christmas. I'm not going to church on Sundays very regularly, but I feel like God is graciously revealing God's self to me through other people and becoming really alive for me in very incarnate, mundane ways, not just in my own head and heart or in my own silent prayers or weak devotional life."

"What are some of those incarnate ways? How is God becoming flesh to you?" she prodded.

"In my friendships—how my girlfriend Sophie listens to me and creates a space for me to share how badly I'm doing whenever I need it. How my friend Nora, who lives in another state, lets me call her in the middle of the night because I can't sleep. And when I take my daily walk, I feel a little put back together at the end of it. It's almost like I'm figuring out that experiencing God's love and presence isn't just about my being obedient and performing well for God. It's simply God's love. It's not about tests and being strong enough and doing whatever it takes to not be rejected by God. It's about love. I know that sounds kooky, but it's what I'm feeling these days and it's kind of a relief."

"It doesn't sound kooky. It sounds like you are letting yourself come to God in a very real and present state of being. That can be a very helpful and sincere way to pray—communicating with God with the real emotions we are feeling and not with pat responses that we think God wants to hear from us. I believe God wants us to learn to voice our hearts honestly before him. Just like the psalmists."

"Say more," I said.

"Well, learning to pray and communicate from the present seat of your emotions is part of learning to be awake and aware of life around you and within you. You are a very intelligent woman, Enuma, but sometimes we can get addicted to our minds just like an alcoholic becomes addicted to the bottle to cope. Sometimes we can overanalyze God's presence in our lives, always looking for signs to interpret. Sometimes the most faithful prayers are the questions we bring to God."

"I never thought about that."

"I want to encourage you to lean into God's peace wherever you find it. God is consistent and generous and abundant in guiding us and in affirming his will with us."

"But what if I relax so much that I miss the signs?" I worried aloud.

"You will not miss the signs. You might choose to ignore them, but you will not miss them. God is too generous with them."

I took exceptional comfort in hearing this from a nun.

✳ ✳ ✳

Over the next year of sessions with Sister Catherine I struggled not to get lost in my head and in my own perspectives of how God works or what God desires of me. I learned to temper my propensity for solitude and quiet with intentional phone calls and visits and walks outside. When I would lose myself to the thoughts of a demanding God who wanted singleness from me despite my wishes. I would make sure to get back into some active way of living in the world. It helped that over the past few months I was learning to let other voices into my head, like Sister Catherine's telling me not to try too hard to squeeze myself into something that didn't seem to be my size. And I learned to recognize that the voice of God can often be identified by the fruit it creates—peace, gentleness, joy, and everything else in Galatians 5. Sister Catherine taught me about how we often relate to God the way we relate in our human relationships. I had a field day with that insight. Man! Perhaps that's another book.

We did eventually talk about the nun thing, and I asked her to share

her story with me, when and how she knew she was called to such a life and what it was like for her. She told me that she knew when she was sixteen and that she just couldn't imagine doing anything else with her life. She shared how disappointed and saddened her parents had been because it meant the end of certain dreams they had for her, like marriage and children. But she couldn't be talked out of it, and when she was eighteen years old, she left her family home and joined the convent.

"Was it ever hard for you? Did you ever regret your choice?" I asked.

I could almost see her thinking back to her youth, the pictures flashing inside her mind like a silent movie. "I don't think I ever regretted it, but it was hard sometimes. I had to learn how to live with other women, some of whom I really didn't like that much, and how to give up a lot of control in my life. That was probably the most difficult thing, not being able to go wherever I wanted when I wanted. You have to remember that when I first became a nun, things were different. We didn't have as much freedom as we do now. But I never felt like there was anything else I wanted to do more than serve God that way. It was a joy even when it was hard."

"Did you ever fall in love?"

She smiled. "Of course I did. I became a nun, not a robot. At one point in my early twenties, I started having feelings for someone, and I had to tell my Superior about it. It was really painful because I knew there was nothing I could do about it. I just had to get over it."

"And you never felt like leaving the sisterhood?"

"Not really. I never had romantic feelings for anyone that seemed to run deeper than what I felt for God. I just couldn't imagine anything bringing more lasting satisfaction. That's just how it was for me."

"Hmm," was all I could say.

"Forget about becoming a nun for just a minute. Tell me how you feel toward God when you think about even just being called to singleness," she said.

"Honestly, the thought of it makes me want to stay away from God. I am so tired and weak right now that I don't even feel capable of discerning anything for myself. I just want to rest this summer, and if I have to address the loss of my father, that is more than enough for me to chew on," I blurted out.

"What else?"

"I feel like I need God's love and comfort more than ever. I want him to be a part of the healing process with my dad. I want to rest in the peace and freedom and love of God and not feel threatened by his love and demands."

"Maybe you should try honoring whatever you are really feeling for a while and share that with God, everything you just shared with me, even the part about wanting to stay away from God. Everyone's call is different, but I imagine that if you were called to be a nun, you would feel excited about the prospect even while aware of the difficulties and sacrifices it would bring. The fact that you have always wanted a husband and children, to build a family, is a calling in itself. Think about that."

✴ ✴ ✴

When I quit church I didn't stop hungering for God. That is a pretty important little tidbit to share. Granted, I wasn't exactly sure what a faithful spiritual life could look like without a home church and traditional faith community to head to every Sunday. But I believed my time with Sister Catherine and everything I was learning was helping me make some headway toward a healthier notion of spiritual community. I had to believe that sometimes God grades us for effort over actual accomplishment. The fact that I still *wanted* to commune with the holy had to count for something. So without really plotting it out, I just started doing whatever did bring me some sense of peace and made me crave more of God— the most encompassing of which was learning to seek out quiet spaces in my daily life. I found myself increasingly aching for silence. I lost most of my desire to watch TV and to listen to music while driving. I can't explain why this happened, but maybe the key point is that I was willing to start listening to what my heart, mind, and spirit seemed to want, not what I assumed was expected of me as a Christian, a seminary-educated one at

that. It wasn't about becoming my own god or anything idolatrous like that. It was just about trying to quiet as much as I could around me, so I could hear the conversations going on within me and around me.

I was going to start listening for God in the mundane cracks and crevices of life. And almost as important, I was going to start being really honest with God about all my feelings! Boldly sharing what I longed for and what was hard for me in faith and life. I was going to practice what I had tried to steer away from during my seminary days: revisiting my *personal relationship with Jesus*! Except that I no longer thought of that relationship as something I did alone, even when I was by myself. I actually took the liberty of believing in the idea of the communion of saints and the cloud of witnesses. I was sort of counting on seeking out a stream of ordinary men and women of faith to journey with me, even though we wouldn't be sharing church pews and weekly bulletins. Some of them might actually be dead like the Trappist monk and writer Thomas Merton, whose writings were teaching me about the holy chaos of conversion and vocation, or the Jewish artist Marc Chagall, whose delight in color and whimsy was just one sacred side of seeking divine gift and stability in a dark and erratic world. I would journey with them through books and images. Others might be alive and thriving like the poet Mary Oliver or my indispensable girlfriends. Yes, it was going to be an experiment, but I figured, what genuine attempt at faithful living isn't?

Chapter 9

Burden-bearing God,
you carry the weight of our failings without
complaint. Teach me to be a burden-bearer for
others and to recognize grace more readily.

I snuck up behind Matt in the linen section of Bed, Bath and Beyond. He was buying a new duvet cover, and Sophie and I had come to help him figure out what he wanted. We decided he wanted a nice shade of gray-blue and some cocoa-colored pillow shams. He only bought the duvet cover. I had a question stewing in my mind all day and I wanted Matt to help me think about it. So I sidled up to him just like that sneaky freaky guy from Seinfeld, "the Sidler," and I whispered, "Matt, I want you to think about this question and offer me some answers before the night is over. What does *grace* mean?"

"Ahh," he said, as though he'd been anticipating my inquisition all along. "And I've got till after dinner, right?"

"Yeah. But you don't have to answer all at once. It can come out in spurts. You know, as you get ideas."

"Oh, thanks," he said rolling his eyes at the ceiling. That was not a very gracious move on Matt's part.

Matt, by the way, is an old classmate of mine from seminary. He's really smart. He not only gets Søren Kierkegaard but he argues with him. Who argues with a nineteenth-century Danish philosopher? Smart people. He's also in a band. Actually it's cooler than that. He's the lead singer of the band he put together called The Prayers and Tears. Matt's music reminds me of a cross between The Smiths and Jeff Buckley, except you can tell Matt's been severely theologically educated. It is his blessing and his curse. His music is lonely, haunting, a wee bit melodramatic

and always makes me want to cry out, "Why, dear God, is life so hard and why must I be plagued with such deep sensitivities that compel me to peer beneath the thin ice-like surface of Western cultural superficiality and consumerism? Why, dear Lord, why?" It also makes me want to read all my old journals from junior high and bawl all over again about why Sam Davidson was not duly smitten with me and my two-toned jeans and studded belts.

"Why do you want to know about grace?" Matt asked me once we'd sat down at the Red Robin. Sophie explained that I was writing a book. I explained that I didn't think I really knew what grace was. Matt explained that maybe that's what I should say in the book. I punched Matt in the face and asked how grace would respond. Just kidding. I would never hurt Matt's face. He has the cutest, slightly alarmed-looking face of a lost little boy who's just written a hit song about being a lost little boy and now doesn't know what to do with all the female attention he's getting. I punched him in the arm. And then I changed the subject. But only after Matt's whole "look at me, I'm an honest Christian" thing was duly noted.

I don't especially understand the concept of grace. My seminary professors never spoke at length about it. It was just assumed that by talking about other doctrines and theological concepts, we somehow would understand what grace was, if we didn't just naturally get it. So I'm still somewhat stuck in the dark about grace. I confuse it with words like *freebie* or *phew* and *get out of jail free card*. Maybe that's not so bad. Maybe I don't have to know what it means. Maybe I just have to receive it. But somehow I'm convinced that getting a better handle on grace will give me a better chance of recognizing where I fail to offer it and for that matter, to receive it.

The catechism of the Catholic Church says that grace is our God-given ability to participate in God's life. God here is understood as Father, Son, and Holy Ghost. That's nice and to the point. But when I think about defining grace, I get muddled and confused about where to start. I begin sweating under my armpits and racking my brain for sentences I must have read from the likes of Thomas Aquinas or Augustine back when I was skimming entire theology books for mid-term exams. But all I can think of are lyrics from that U2 song conveniently called "Grace" that compare this Christian ideology to a simple girl bearing creation on her, I assume fertile, life-giving hips. Whenever I hear those lines I immediately imagine a West African woman wearing the traditional colorful daily garb of ethnic wrap skirt and loose-fitting top; she has a young child wrapped around her hips with what should be her head scarf. I grew up seeing women carry their young to and from the local market. I am taken by the notion that God's grace might be symbolized by a West African woman off to market bearing the burden and humanity of the world as her child. Maybe this is because I was raised by beautiful West African women— my mother and countless aunts, whose colorful and passionate person- alities seemed larger than life. These women danced freely and sensually at family gatherings, trying to teach me how to sway my hips with what should have been a natural rhythmic instinct. These were women who weren't afraid to discipline me and advise me as though they themselves had given birth to me. These were women who, in my mind's eye, could do just about anything: shake the equivalent of a dollar out of a quarter, balance full-time work and child-rearing, and find enough time to travel the world—coming back home with pockets full of unbelievable stories that suggested they had visited countries that didn't exist to the rest of us. And somehow that U2 song makes me imagine *grace* as a passion- ate, colorful, endlessly resourceful and imaginative West African woman, strong and playful but full of loving discipline and sage counsel. Maybe "grace" never runs out of imaginative ways to love us and to encourage us to choose life over all other options no matter how dire and desperate things may seem.

I know I should here insert some cultural commentary about how U2 is replacing the church fathers in teaching young people about faith and justice and love and stuff, but I'm not enough of a critic to do all that. I mean, let's get real: who doesn't love U2? Young, old, wise and fool- ish, half-dead and barely alive, everyone loves U2. I especially love U2. In fact, I believe I am their biggest fan, and I would love to join them on

their next trip to save people in Africa, or if they ever have to meet with Johnny Depp for any particular reason (in case you're reading this, Bono). I could be their translator for their time with Johnny, since I am very fluent in understanding hotness. But I digress.

I'm used to clichéd semidefinitions of grace tossed out in conversation by members of my socioeconomic club: "It's only by God's grace you and I weren't born in Darfur," or "It's only by God's grace we weren't on that flight." But if grace is about life with God, then such definitions don't make any sense. It would seem that only by God's grace would we be able to consider the people and plight of Darfur as our people and our own plight. It is only by God's grace that we make our way to serve at homeless shelters, to hold vigil at state prison execution sites, to stop buying things we don't need and to start imagining our world beyond national borders. But grace has also got to manifest itself in other ways because I've experienced it, and I haven't really experienced the other stuff I just preached about, you know, the vigils and stuff. And grace surely has something to do with the fact that God still has some use for me who shies away from homeless shelters and prison vigils. Maybe grace fills our lives in manageable doses because too much of a good thing could kill us. Kind of like not being able to peer into the brilliance of the sun without getting our retinas burned off.

So a large part of the grace I currently identify with is about humility and gaining perspective, realizing that it's God alone who keeps us connected to any community of saints, who guides our hearts even when we rebelliously take strange sabbaticals, who lets us join in the work of God, and who helps us learn to see one another with a bit more humility and awe. Grace is how God uses our grotesquely misguided attempts at goodness and love to channel some word about redemption and hope. And in the midst of channeling these words, we get deeply transformed in ways we could not have conjured up ourselves.

Chapter 10

Disarmed God,
you make yourself vulnerable out of love for
creation. Thank you for people who disarm
themselves and love me by letting me into their
vulnerable spaces.

I met Michael during my church sabbatical and well after I'd put together my "list" of what I was looking for in a boyfriend: tall, handsome, intelligent, Christian, funny, thinks I'm amazing, and has never daydreamt about Halle Berry or supermodel Gisele Bündchen. You know, the usual compatibility traits. "Recovering alcoholic" was not on the list. But Michael seemed to fit everything else, and I hadn't encountered a man so into me since my last nocturnal fantasy about Leonardo DiCaprio (which wouldn't have worked out anyway considering the fact he dated Ms. Bündchen. My guess is he apparently has "daydreamt" about her. Did I mention that I am a sucker for E! Entertainment Television and trashy magazines?) The funny thing is that when I found out Michael liked me, I mean "liked me, liked me," the first words out of my mouth were, "Shit, that's the last thing I need." Not because he was a recovering alcoholic; I didn't know that then. But because I already had my hands full with a melodramatic friendlationship with another extremely hot man of God, Dean, who lived in a converted barn in the country and with whom I would read poetry and eat strawberries and tabbouleh and have intense conversations about death and resurrection. It was every bit as pretentious as it sounds, but he sure was dreamy, and I thought I had found my soul mate, my mildly rebellious wild-haired philosophy-reading evangelical Christian who looked like he'd just stepped off a stoop in Greenwich Village and straight into a Levi jeans commercial. Just one look at him confirmed to me that this was God's will. Life in Durham was looking up.

Michael, on the other hand, was classically handsome with kind eyes and instant charm. You knew right away that most people loved him at first sight—parents, teachers, and all the girls he'd left behind in sunny California. Michael also loved Jesus, but he didn't read philosophy. He read Hunter S. Thompson books. He watched *South Park* and played soccer and lent his pickup truck to anyone who asked.

Things didn't work out with Dean. One night we sat across from each other at a wood table in the darkest corner of the smoke-filled Federal Bar in downtown Durham. Over glasses of ale we exchanged poems explaining how we had each processed the whole friendlationship. Basically, he "pocketed my smile," and I let him "seep in like rain through cracks." Then I went on a date with Michael. We got ice cream at Ben and Jerry's and I felt like I'd known him my whole life.

I will never be able to find the words to explain how soul-expanding it was to be in a relationship with Michael. Every man I ever date from now on should offer up their complimentary bag of peanuts on Michael's behalf because the gem they will receive in me is in some small part due to how Michael and I rubbed off on each other and created entirely different angles to our personalities, smoothing down some surfaces and sharpening certain edges to withstand a bit more of life's roughhousing. Michael was a man deeply aware of his faults and openly dependent on God. At an early stage of our relationship he told me that he'd always felt like he was sitting in a wheelbarrow on a taut tightrope several hundred feet above the ground, suspended between two cliffs. A precarious situation if it weren't for the added fact that he also always felt that God was pushing the wheelbarrow across the tightrope. Later I called my old college girlfriend Amy, who lives in Minnesota and works as an illustrator, to paint the scene as one might find it in a children's book. I framed the painting and gave it to Michael for our first Christmas together. Even though I felt like I'd always known him and I enjoyed all our early dates, it took me several months to fall in love with Michael. And I can't name the place or the time. It was just several little things that tapped on the outside of my heart until he'd tap-danced his way into the very center.

Mostly it was his patience with me and with life. He would always say that anything really good was worth waiting for, so he was especially willing to wait for me to think through what I wanted from him and our growing relationship. He seemed to know without much explanation that trust was something I struggled with, and letting people into my life beyond a surface level didn't come easily for me. So he waited. He took most things in life one day at a time, a constant reminder to me to stay open to God's surprises and to welcome God's grace. And all the while he showed me who he was, a man who invited homeless men into his house without giving it a second thought, a man who offered his own bed to tired and depressed fellow students for days on end while he slept on the couch, a man who still laughed at fart noises and ate cheese with absolutely everything. When I asked Michael a serious question, he would tell me he had to think about it; days later, out of the blue, he would offer up his answer. Without even knowing it, he taught me a little more about being kinder to strangers and more compassionate toward people whose wounds were not visible on first encounters. And through the stories of his past and the demons he constantly battled he taught me about humility, about sharing the darker corners of life, about confession and repentance and the constant awareness of standing before God by grace alone. And that's how I fell in love with him, beautiful bright blue-eyed, generous recovering alcoholic and all. But somewhere along our time together, he stopped being in recovery, and I found myself in love with a struggling alcoholic. And I began wondering if there was room in that wheelbarrow for two.

God's light shines especially bright through the multiple and endless fragmented slices that exist in broken people. And the more rays of light, the more people are touched. But no one expects such light to come from a broken image. I learned to understand the radical beauty of God through Michael's shards. I learned to begin to acknowledge the beauty of God through my own brokenness.

If you have never experienced the effects of addiction I am not sure how to describe to you what it is like being in relationship with an alcoholic. I could use words like *chaos, random, roller coaster, gaping, long, bewildered, desperate*, and maybe you could say, "Oh, that makes sense. I see where she's going with this." But what if I added a few more words like, *awe, gratitude, revelation, humility*, and yes, *grace*? Would you know where I was going then? Would you have been able to tell me that falling in love with a person of faith who happened to struggle with alcohol addiction and other self-destructive habits would be an invitation into the life of God? Because I would not have believed you. But that is part of the grace I do understand, the grace catching us in the direst of circumstances, in the corners where we seem certain God has left the building. Being with Michael taught me that love and honesty are always tied to grace, like streamers on the back of a newlywed couple's car. Grace is not about being perfect or pushing others to be perfect. It's more about patience, acceptance, and a willingness to see individuals for who they are in Christ and as they stand alone, with all their disheveled parts messing up the pretty picture. It's so much less about "what's in it for me" and so much more about the transformation that happens in us and between us that helps us spill our lives, somewhat clumsily, outside the boundaries we've comfortably drawn around ourselves. While I struggled to love Michael for who he was and not "in spite of" or "because," my understanding of how God loves me was altered. I understand a little bit more now about a love that frees me up to be who I am, disheveled in the most obscure places and endlessly trying to straighten things out. And I do believe that God still wants us to at least work at getting our shit together. Michael taught me the strange beauty of returning again and again before God for another shot at life.

* * *

There wasn't much to say as we drove the hour-long trip to the facility. We had been together for three years, and I knew that this was a big step for Michael, but I hadn't quite figured out what kind of step it was for me. I just knew I had to be there. I turned to face him as he drove. "How are you feeling?" I asked.

"I'm all right. I'm kind of scared."

"I know you are. It makes sense. I'm really proud of you for doing this." I reached out and touched his arm.

He smiled weakly with gratitude. "Thanks so much for coming with me. It means a lot."

"Did you pack everything you need?"

"I think so. It's only a month, and I guess I can do laundry there."

"Well, if you find out you forgot anything, just call me and I'll try and bring it down."

"Thanks, Numey."

I turned to stare out my window and put my face into the breeze. It was a beautiful early summer day and a quiet drive through farmland and two-lane highways. There wasn't much on my mind. It felt quiet in there too. I was scared for him but I knew this was necessary. I couldn't name anything I was feeling about myself. I just kept my face in the wind for a while longer until we pulled up to the gates of the facility.

He pulled the truck into a parking spot, turned off the engine, and we just sat there.

"I can't believe we're here," I said.

"I know."

There was silence. I felt water gathering at the corners of my eyes. "Can we pray together?" I asked.

"That would be great." He took my hands in his like we always did when we prayed, and I offered up the words I found somewhere in my heart. I prayed that God would be with him in a profound way. I prayed for courage to fight demons and for a desire for healing.

Then we got out of the car. I walked with him into the main receiving room which looked like the lobby of a three-star hotel. I sat down and flipped through magazines as the attendant asked Michael to empty his pockets, leave his luggage at the desk, and follow the nurse for his check-in ritual.

* * *

I had broken up with Michael two months before he checked himself into rehab. It was his first and only time, and I made the car trip with him, listened to him tell me he was scared of the next month, and prayed with him in the car. Then I drove myself the hour-ride home, feelings of relief and longing blowing through the cracked windows of the car. In the past three years I had learned more about addiction, grace, divine love, and divine surprise than I ever imagined possible. Michael is a Christian, with a heart big enough to hold the moon. He taught me to open my life to depths of hospitality and humility I hadn't known without him. But no one had taught me what to do with a Christian openly struggling with addiction. No one taught me how to carry another's burdens with love and responsibility the way God carries the burdens of the world on her hips like an ever-nurturing mother.

I want to find a church that teaches me something about carrying each other's burdens, about living into the gift of God's grace so we are free to be the persons and community God calls us to be. I want a church that teaches me to find joy in the somewhat disjointed experiences of life, because in God I understand there is no rush to get healed and perfect this side of heaven. Perhaps freedom in Christ is freedom from the modern pressures to have life figured out by a certain time. And maybe it's grace that will eventually help me to look at God's flawed community; and, instead of washing my hands of it, I will participate in it because I know God is at work there the same way he's at work in my own flawed life. Maybe I love the image of U2's "Grace" because it reminds me that God our mother eternally supports and nourishes us and, most importantly, does not punish us for being the needy creatures God created us to be. The Spirit is the gift of God in us that enables us to see our need as a gift in itself.

I don't imagine that I extended grace to Michael. That would be presumptuous. Rather we both got caught up in the delicate but strong grip of God's grace, that sense of divine love extending outside of God's self and demanding humility from whoever falls into its arms. Only when we find ourselves caught in the arms of grace are we able to extend our own arms out in love toward the other. We see then that no one has received God's love through merit. My full relationship with Michael helped me find God in the reality of earthly living, the mess and disappointments and fractures of life. That is where God is, in those places of human brokenness and failed efforts of being good in the way that God alone is good. I too am broken, and I saw that in slices of my relationship with Michael— the dark pride that blinds me to the community of God. Yet God is gracious and patient and kind and present in our failings and our longings and our hopes and attempts at right living. I pray to learn to sit with this new insight for a while, the reality of being imperfect and broken and still loved by God and still capable of some faithful actions.

Part Two

The Space Between

Chapter 11

Retreating God,
even you took time to rest, to step back from the
crowds and the noise, to find moments of stillness
and silence. I am made in your image.

Hope has walls, even though sometimes our arms don't seem long enough to reach them. But that's when I think God stretches us, and when our fingertips brush up against the surface of hope, we find out that it's soft in some places and hard in others. We find out that the walls of hope are textured and that leaning against them can be both comfortable and painful. Then the walls push out a little more and we're ready for more stretching.

* * *

Breaking up with Michael that summer was hard for a million reasons. One minor one was that if ever I could have used a supportive boyfriend, it was then. A month earlier I had left my full-time job as director of a theological writing center at a top-notch divinity school. I didn't have a new job lined up. And I wasn't planning on getting a new job, at least not the normal 9-to-5 kind of job with benefits and quirky colleagues with whom one could commiserate about how awful the normal benefit-paycheck-giving job was. No, not I. I was going to wing it for a year and see if I really believed that I was called to be a writer and if it really could be true that God supported such a crazy career move. I also felt the need for a year of physical and spiritual renewal, to gather the pieces of myself that had slowly fallen off, like the leaves of a mildly watered basil plant left in the shade with only glimpses of light. That sounds a little dramatic, but it was true. The salary was okay and the benefits were good, but the work was not enough to stimulate my creative energies, while it was busy enough to sap me of any creativity at the end of the day. I also knew it was time to leave because in the office I was left to my own devices with no one to challenge my efforts, foster my growth, or acknowledge my gifts. Sophie and I talked about how expectations can play such a defining and subtle role in human development. I sensed I was losing a little bit of my spirit each day. I needed to write, to try my hand at the passions for reading and creativity that have sustained me since my childhood, always reminding me that I did indeed have passions.

When I told people I was taking a year off for physical and spiritual renewal, to read and write, to remember the parts of me I loved and wanted to nourish, to pray with a companion for a year, and to discern which ways God wanted this particular branch of his to grow, people asked me what I planned to do with myself. No one really wanted to give me permission to live a year of my life with such seemingly elusive motives. The questioning suggested that such a venture was impractical, irresponsible, navel-gazing at best, and a luxury I couldn't afford. They were right about not being able to afford it, but my spirit told me I couldn't afford to do otherwise.

I was feeling somewhat lost to myself. My three-year relationship was ending, my work environment was stealing away any sense of creativity and passion I had toward the idea of vocation, and I was deeply out of rhythm with my spiritual life. There were no spiritual markers to my days: no morning prayer, no praise songs, no closing of the day before God. I wasn't praying with anyone on a regular basis, and I definitely wasn't reading the Bible. You have to understand, these had once been typical activities in my life, back whenever it was that I considered myself somewhat spiritually healthy. Now, I was very aware of feeling "lost at sea" without any kind of anchor in sight. My spirit felt desperately ill, and I needed to work on my relationship with God. Sure, there were a million reasons why I was spiritually out of whack and playing "Pin the Tail on the Deity," but at that point in my life it seemed most tied to a yearning for vocational discernment. After about six months of sitting with the idea of quitting my job and taking a year to regroup vocationally, spiritually, and emotionally, I did it. I gave my notice and stared ahead at an unknown year of being at home, self-employed and the guardian of my own time. I was scared shitless, but I couldn't wait. Since I was also officially taking a guilt-free break from church, I was hungry for a game of hide-and-seek with the Spirit, curious to find her in all sorts of hidden corners of daily life in the world—baking bread, walking, looking at art, reading poetry, and even in exploring my passion for writing.

✳ ✳ ✳

For the first two months I tried to find a routine to fall into, fumbling a bit without structure to my days. Some habits started sneaking into place, like walking my dog, Bella, midmorning after her post-breakfast nap and my coffee and mumbled prayers. We'd hike a hilly three-mile trail each day, familiarizing ourselves a little more with the dips and turns of the forest floor. I was learning to ration my gait just after a mile and a quarter, in time to tackle the steepest part of the course; and Bella was learning that chasing squirrels was not conducive to her health. I quickly grew to cherish those walks, to crave the time when my only activity was to pace my steps, to notice the parts of my body that ached or seemed to be strengthening, and to find such satisfaction in the cold flow of drinking water at the end of the trail. I thought a lot during these walks, or maybe *mused* is a better word. I mused over whatever terrain my mind wandered into, spontaneous prayers for a friend in another state, chasing ideas for writing, imagining the lives of the few people who passed us by on the trail, and wondering about the life of trees and how much snapped trunks looked like wounded human limbs.

The afternoons went by quickly. I was writing curriculum for various publishing houses, and the deadlines kept me focused on living one week at a time. It was a gift to work from home, to be eking out some sort of living by doing what I loved—struggling with words and articulating faith. I pretty much lived from hand to mouth, conscious that being single and childless made this adventure somewhat more feasible. I felt fortunate for having this time, and I wasn't going to take it for granted. Instead, I steeped myself in it, in the quiet of my home, in the freedom of my days, in the spaces to cry or pray or gaze as needed. I gave my imagination and my spirit permission to run wild during that year, to dream boldly, to confess my longings and desires to God without apology, and to openly acknowledge my times of spiritual sloth and struggle those many mornings when I resisted prayer or church.

I was also learning to be single again. After Michael came home from rehab, we worked on maintaining a friendship. We had been through too much to just call it complete quits. It was not an easy thing to do, but we were open to learning as we went. The most difficult thing for me were the daily, minute reminders that I was no longer part of a twosome. It's very much like that overused analogy of losing a limb but still feeling an itch or an ache for a while. Except, unlike losing an appendage, this also felt strangely freeing. I wanted to return to so much of what I had with Michael not only because I deeply loved him but also just out of habit of being so wrapped up in another person's life. Missing him—missing us—was punctuated with growing affirmations of having made the best decision in light of both our lives. But even healthy change can be difficult and can take getting used to.

It wasn't going to be an easy year on any other account either. That became clear very quickly. Some days were full of nothing but stress. No amazing walks with my dog, no mindless gazing at the blowing leaves, just stress over not knowing when the next paycheck would come for work I had already completed. And often I was as busy as when I had a full-time job! This year of spiritual and physical renewal wasn't going to work if I didn't think consciously about the jobs I accepted, the things I did with my time, and whether or not I walked every day. It was going to be a hard year, and I knew without a doubt I wouldn't be doing it for any longer than that. I missed having a regular paycheck and health insurance. I had to do so much writing, juggling multiple deadlines just to barely make ends meet. All these frustrations and the sense of isolation surprised me. It was like spending my days on silent retreat without the benefit of spiritual renewal. I had to keep reminding myself that this was what I wanted—time to myself to write and think and read. Except that having all this new time alone also reminded me how much I ached for community and how much it didn't seem like I had much, if any. Although I had wonderful individual friends, I lacked a community of people who knew and cared for one another and were intent on bearing one another's burdens and calling forth emotional and spiritual growth, like a church or a family—healthy ones anyway.

✳ ✳ ✳

On some mornings I woke up full of gratitude for the healing I was experiencing, and I remembered to believe in God's faithfulness. I didn't know what the year would bring, but something made me feel my leap of faith would be blessed. Rereading Kathleen Norris's *The Quotidian Mysteries*, I was freshly reminded of the call of daily life and the need for ritual and routine that speaks to the beautiful mundaneness of things. We are called to live out the Incarnation in the ordinary time of our lives. That is what liturgy is—the repetition of words and actions that praise God and form us into life-giving creatures. I was gracefully reminded of the need for liturgy even when I didn't feel like going to church, and that habits shape us even when we don't recognize the transformation taking place. Trying to live a liturgical life, one that honors life's earnest rhythms of celebrating joy, painful longing, and ordinary grace takes courage because it calls us from our little worlds to believe that we are not at the center. The reality is that our woes and troubles are not the end of things. Christ is the end of things, and Christ has released us from the burden of believing we call the shots in life.

I fell into the habit of reading poems over breakfast, a discipline that helped me enter each new day by slowing down my mind and my confusion enough to look for truth in small collections of words. It was like a daily invitation to attend to life, to listen and perceive and imagine. The collection of poems that fed my spirit the most during that time was Mary Oliver's *Thirst*. So fitting. She writes of grief and of finding faith in the daily while embracing her grief over the loss of her partner. It is beautiful writing, and it helped me name and accept that in the midst of receiving the gifts of my off-year I was still dealing with my own grief, of leaving a structured work environment, of being without a church community, and of letting go of Michael. It is hard to reconstruct a life after a breakup from someone you loved deeply. The companionship and intimacy born in a loving relationship is such a gift. It is reassuring to me that at the beginning of Creation, God was sensitive enough to know that a man or woman alone is lonely, that humans need one another. It made me feel as though God knew my heartache over that loss.

I've come to think of this period of my life as the space between. Only back then, I wasn't terribly certain what I was in between. I knew what I'd left behind, but I couldn't convince you that I was clear on where I was headed. And somehow that was okay. I was learning some new things about myself; at least I was learning how to articulate some of the things I suppose I have always known—that too much social interaction over-stimulates me and makes it difficult for me to navigate the ensuing days, and that silence is the sound I prefer the most, with classical music a close second. I've come to understand the importance of owning and accepting these mini self-revelations. I imagine and hope this knowledge will make me a more faithful person, that establishing needed boundaries is deeply related to keeping the faith. So during that time between I was learning to create better boundaries and to surround myself with sounds that healed, nourished, and inspired me. My other realization was that very few people in my personal life at that time had a calming presence. I was craving more people like that and playfully considered putting an ad out on Craigslist.

Chapter 12

So I had more or less just willingly turned my life a wee bit upside down. But not everything changed. I was still deeply thirsty for God. I knew I wanted to start reading the Bible again, but I didn't know where I wanted to start. The mere thought of starting at Genesis and working my way through seemed overwhelming. I started by nibbling my way through the Psalms. I reasoned that if I couldn't connect with people in the pews, I'd try to reconnect with the prayers and praises of the psalmists. I found myself strangely comforted just reading the earnest sincere offerings of people who also hungered for God, who sinned against God, and who yearned for forgiveness. Reading the Psalms allowed me to grow into my own haphazard prayers and to inch my way before God with all my conflicting thoughts and feelings. If people in the Bible could shake their fists at God while truly believing in the majesty of God, then maybe there was room in my own faith for anger and frustration, sorrow and questioning, bafflement and longing. Maybe there was room to sit in pain, to beseech God, and to plead with God. And still find some corners to crawl into after it's all said and done and lift my hands in praise and gratitude that I worship a God who can take all this and more if need be.

* * *

You've probably guessed that my prayer life is sporadic at best, but once in a while the Holy Ghost gets a hold of me and I fall into a seasoned

trance of regular prayer time either alone or with my girlfriends. I like to imagine I had something to do with the birth of Sophie's son, David, because we prayed for his conception every week for about six months before Sophie got pregnant. He might have been a glint in Daddy' eye, but I helped bring him more clearly into the picture. One day I'll tell him that and he'll regret all those times he acted out while I tried to talk on the phone with his mother.

I missed having a prayer partner, so eventually I asked my girlfriend Liz if she would be interested in meeting with me once a week to pray together. I confessed that I had no real idea what this might look like and suggested that we just show up and kinda see what happened. Liz is very type-A. All Liz's ducks are in a row and they are alphabetized by name. But Liz said yes to my loosey-goosey, nonstructured stab at regular prayer. I figured that was a sign that the good Lord was willing and the creek wouldn't rise.

The thing with prayer is that it's hard to get into and hard to stick with. Sometimes I come to prayer feeling muddled and not knowing where to start. Is it okay to start with what I want, or do I have to fish around God with compliments about how awesome God is? It's strange business trying to know the proper prayer etiquette. I know Jesus taught us how to pray with the Lord's Prayer, but sometimes that doesn't seem enough. It doesn't feel like I really got my point across or really expressed how badly I need God's help. Though I have to confess, as much as I hate to admit it, I sometimes channel God's grace through unanswered prayers, or rather prayers that God seems to say no to with softly slamming doors.

I've been thinking lately about the things I pray about. I always feel like I have to couch my words very carefully so it doesn't sound like I'm being totally selfish and asking for the wrong thing. Sort of like I assume that what I want could never be what God wants for me. That can't be completely right, right? I mean, I know I have a bad case of original sin, so that trickles down to me not really knowing what's best for me, blah, blah, blah, but why do I just assume that when it comes to my personal life I never know the right things for which to pray? It's like there are these shelves stocked and labeled with appropriate prayer topics. When it's time to pray, open your prayer closet and pick an item: World Peace, Middle East Violence, African Children, Natural Disasters, Cures and Miracle Healings for Terminal Illnesses, The Homeless. There's no guilt associated with praying for these things, but why do I always feel guilty praying for my own longings? Is there room in the closet for Amazing Girl Desires Mate or Woman with Ticking Clock Hungers for Child or even Weary, Navel-gazing Christian Longs for Thriving Church Community? I hear this little voice inside my head saying, *How can you love God if you don't pray endlessly for foreign countries and hungry people you've never met?* How can I, people? How can I?

✳ ✳ ✳

Liz and I started getting together on Friday mornings. Our structure found itself—gripe, gossip, share recent joys and aches, and eventually pray. I think God likes it when we pray together because we tend to giggle a lot—actually, *cackle* is a more fitting word. Sometimes I worry God won't take our prayers seriously if they are sprinkled with laughter. I have to trust God's got a sense of humor. But life with God is not always a laughing matter. In fact, I've been starting to feel a little slighted by God. It seemed like it was always my girlfriends' prayers getting answered and not mine. Sophie got the kid, Liz's broken heart was just out of reconstructive surgery, and here I was, still waiting to cash in my holy chips.

The other day I confided in Liz about my less-than-amicable feelings toward the Lord Almighty.

"So, I'm thinking of the best way to put this," I said.

"To put what?"

"How I'm feeling toward God. I mean about the whole job thing. I've been thinking about going back to normal work, and I thought I'd found the perfect match for me. I prayed so earnestly about it. I even enlisted the prayer reserves and called out people to stand vigil with me. What else could I have done?"

"Enuma, I know how much you wanted that position. It's okay to be angry with God."

"It's not so much that I'm angry. I just feel like, like—okay this is going to sound kind of weird but whatever. I just feel like God is kind of like a husband who lives in the house with me, and even though I love him deeply and definitely want him around, I don't feel like speaking to him right now. I'm a little irritated, and I want him to do his thing in one room while I do my thing in the other. But it's not like there's any real reason for me to be upset with him, I just am."

"What if God is a woman? Does that make God your wife and you a lesbian?" Liz asked. It sounded like the kind of smart-ass thing I'd say.

"Liz, are you even listening to me?"

"Umm, yeah, and it sounds kind of like anger. I mean, I think you're justified in being upset—not at God but at the situation. Don't feel bad about it. You really wanted to work for the Global Office, and it seemed like a perfect fit. Even if it meant you moving to New York."

I snorted and mused aloud, "Yeah, I can totally hear a therapist's voice in my holy matrimony with the 'Savior of the world'—'*Really, Enuma, it doesn't matter whether it's right or not, just let the Savior know how you feel.*'"

Sometimes I wonder about prayer—why we do it, if it even works, or if it's just a matter of playing the lottery—sometimes you win, sometimes you don't.

* * *

I am starting to think there's a connection between my inability to pray honestly and my struggle to share my vulnerabilities and needs in relationships. My girlfriend Madeline lost her husband to cancer four years into their marriage and nine days before the birth of their first child. He was thirty years old. About a year later, Madeline told me that she had stopped going to church. Not because she had given up on God but because church didn't feel authentic anymore. As she put it, "Everyone is too grateful." She confessed to me how the devastating loss of her husband had made her experience church differently, noticing what was lacking in the midst of her deep needs for authentic and messy faith that matched the reality of her messy life.

"I never realized until now how no one ever offers up to God their prayers of anger," she said. "The prayers of the people never include space for those of us who want to honestly and openly acknowledge that life can be unbearably painful. Sometimes what we need are prayers that say, 'God, I'm angry. Help me live into that anger in a healthy way. Help me be patient with you and with myself and with the shittiness of life. Help me stop crying for answers when you know I will never have answers. Help me learn to live for just today with the things I can't understand.' No one ever prays about anger."

* * *

What would my life be like if I just stopped praying altogether? I mean, what if God promised me that things would stay the same regardless of whether I prayed or not: would I still continue to pray? That's a hard question. But I've thought about it because on a whole other level I'm a little curious about why some of us feel compelled to pray, even when our scales of belief are tipped toward the negative. But even with a sporadic prayer life, I can't imagine a life without prayer, without some effort to reach for God with all the cares and worries I drag with me wherever I go, and without some effort to invite God to speak to me in the times when I am sensible enough to just be quiet. Plus there's a side of me that doesn't really know how to express my love for God without prayer in my life. I'm not sure when or how I started feeling this way, but somewhere along the line, I've discovered that when I do pray, I am reminded of who God is and who I am. It's hard to pray for anything without at some point naming God as one who is capable of all things. And it's hard to say thanks without at some point naming God as one who gives generously and without merit. So I'm clued in that prayer is not just a means to an end but actually shapes how I think about God and my own place in the world

and in relation to others. Prayer is as much about God and community as it is about my human needs, and that's also part of why I feel both guilty and out of sorts when I am not fostering a regular prayer life.

I catch myself thinking about the characters in the Old Testament and wondering what kind of prayer warriors they were. The first names that come to mind are David, Moses, and Abraham. All three of those guys seemed to be so close to God, and I can only imagine such closeness had to involve regular communication with God. And not only prayers of praise and thanksgiving but also a genuine relationship that involved shaking fists and questioning and not listening, saying I'm sorry and being forgiven. I have to believe that was also a part of what got communicated between these guys and God. Knowing the stories of these men, I also have to believe that a real and ongoing prayer life can lead to uncomfortable life situations. I am not sure how I feel about that. Actually, I am sure—I don't like it. But I can't know about all aspects of such an intimate relationship with the Divine without having that level of connection. Maybe Moses going to free the Israelites, or David slaying Goliath, or Abraham walking with Isaac up that mountain was nuanced with graces and trust I know nothing about. In any case, I may have been in a season of unstructured prayer during my time between, but it didn't mean I stopped communicating with God or that I lost my desire to do so. I just started thinking about new ways to travel that path.

Chapter 13

As a kid, one of my favorite Christmas carols was "We Three Kings." And now as an adult, one of my favorite times of year is the season of Epiphany, the time of year when the church marks the visitation of the magi, those wise men who followed a star all the way to the baby Jesus who had been born in a stable. It starts on January 6 but, depending on your tradition, lasts a day, a week, or right up until Ash Wednesday.

Because I love this time, I extend it as long as I can. I'm not sure what it is that draws me to this season. Maybe it's the mysteriousness of the wise men that intrigues me, the fact that they were astrologers who navigated their lives by reading the stars. I think of the wise men as somewhat saintly, sexy, intellectual, dark-haired manly men who traveled with amazing fragrances and spices and could really defend themselves in a desert brawl. I also imagine this mysterious sensitive side to them. Any man who follows the stars and listens to the voice of God has got to be a bit romantic, don't you think? But I digress. I know why I love Epiphany: it is a season of light and guidance and revelation. Epiphany makes me believe God wants to show up in the most surprising but gift-filled spaces of life, spaces where we never imagine we might find God. That thought is both beautiful and reassuring to me.

So during my space-between year I decided to try and pray into the different ecclesial seasons, wondering how my exterior life might be shaped if my interior life was in sync with the rhythmic ticking of Christian liturgical time keeping. Throughout Epiphany I sought to live into

the season of revelation. I started by reading Matthew 2:1-12, the biblical narrative upon which Epiphany is based. I made note of central themes: pilgrimage, journeying, searching, divine guidance, revelation, gift giving, gift receiving, worship, recognition of Christ, divine protection, and returning home by another way. Then I spent my days thinking, writing, and praying about how each theme might apply to my life at the moment. I prayed especially for guidance and wisdom to see more clearly.

✳ ✳ ✳

It had been months since I'd spoken with my girlfriend Bea. She lives in California, and during that time of my life it was terribly hard to stay connected to people who weren't within a fifteen-mile radius of me. Some might have called me depressed. Okay, some did. I preferred to think of it as cocooning. That's what it felt like. Something within me knew this season couldn't last forever, but while it did last, my focus was my internal life. I honestly didn't think I could move forward without going through whatever I was going through. I had to ride it out while doing the seemingly self-indulgent work of actively listening to my life. Anyway, one afternoon during Epiphany I called Bea. She and I have one of those friendships that can pick up wherever we left off. She is also one of the few friends whom I trust for spiritual wisdom.

I told Bea that I felt barren. That even though I was halfway through my intentional year, my life seemed empty and I couldn't produce anything meaningful. All I wanted to do was walk my dog, sleep in, and stare at the little pond in my backyard. I confessed that I felt spiritually empty most of the time and very uncertain about what the next vocational stage should be for me. *Barrenness* was the one word that expressed what I felt because I wanted to create a new life in so many ways.

"I think you should read Isaiah 54 and pray through it," she said.

"Why? What's it about?"

"It's about God's faithfulness and presence in the middle of what seems like hopelessness. God compares Israel to a barren woman."

That evening I turned out the lights in my bedroom, lit a candle, and sat on the floor. I opened my Bible to Isaiah chapter 54.

"Sing, O barren one who did not bear;
burst into song and shout,
you who have not been in labor!
For the children of the desolate woman will be more
than the children of her that is
married, says the LORD."

Now I am sensible enough to know not to play Russian roulette with the Word of God, imagining that I can take any verse and apply it to the circumstances of my life and look for how God must definitely be speaking to me. I know that every part of scripture is part of a larger whole and that this verse was intended for a people, for a community, not for an individual Christian sitting alone in her room in North America. But I also know that God is a God beyond limitations and that part of the gift of Gentiles, like me, being grafted into the Israelite covenant is that my faith story cannot be separated from the Israelite story. The God of Abraham, Isaac, and Jacob is also the God incarnate in Christ. By my baptism into Christ I have also been baptized into the wider story. I am just trying to say that it was deeply comforting to read the words of Isaiah and to remember that spiritual barrenness runs in the family.

I sat in the candlelit room quietly telling God how I felt, naming the spaces of barrenness in my life, and praying for new life to take root in me, life blessed by God, whatever that might look like. And I prayed for what I thought God wanted me to give birth to—a more fruitful writing life, a clearer sense of vocation, a larger heart capable of holding both joy and sorrow, and a healed imagination.

The following evening a few girlfriends came over to my house to help me celebrate my thirty-fourth birthday. My girlfriend Michelle handed me a gift and a card and said she had bought the gift last summer in South Africa, but she thought I should have it now. I opened the card

first and read with gaping mouth, "Happy Birthday Enuma. Your life is pregnant with possibilities." Then I opened the gift. It was a brightly colored painting of a pregnant African woman, her belly protruding from the center of the canvas. I looked at Michelle in disbelief, dumbfounded at the playfulness of God, and all I could say was, "You have no idea what this means to me."

* * *

I continued to mark time by the liturgical calendar. February brought the end of Epiphany and the beginning of Lent, and I tried to find a new rhythm for prayer, to shape my words and actions according to the contours of Lent. I began praying to learn to discipline my impulsive desires, even the good desires, to learn that it is okay to not have everything I want. It is okay to consume less in a variety of ways. It is okay to curb one's pleasurable activities for a season. I felt led to reflect on the rhythm of fasting and feasting in my own life and to find faithful ways of engaging the world. Yet despite my valiant efforts, I have to admit the year continued to be a difficult one. I struggled with God and God's seeming absence. Sophie tried to encourage me by telling me how much she really believed God was at work in my life, even though she couldn't explain why I was going through what I was going through. She told me not to be afraid to stick my hand in there—into the darkness—and feel around for whatever it was God wanted me to pull out of this experience. It sounded scary but seemed like a worthwhile thing to do. I just felt so undone. There were no railings for me to hold onto anywhere.

During Easter I began to meet with three friends once a week to practice *lectio divina*, the ancient art of meditating on scripture passages and listening for God's voice communally. One morning we read through the Road to Emmaus passage, where Jesus walks unidentified with the two disciples as they converse about what has just happened to Jesus—his death and burial. One of my girlfriends commented on how she went about praying to pray by asking questions of Jesus and having Jesus ask questions of her. It can be difficult but maybe our task is to whittle out comfort from asking Christ hard questions and receiving questions in response. In the midst of the disciples' grief and deep longing, Jesus comes and what had seemed impossible is suddenly possible. Maybe to be Easter people means we expect our hopes to be realized but allow Christ room to alter what those hopes look like. Maybe hope has to engage despair and re-narrate it.

* * *

Bea also suggested that I read the book *When the Heart Waits: Spiritual Direction for Life's Sacred Questions* by Sue Monk Kidd, which turned out to be a lifeline in my sea of desperation and confusion. Kidd narrates her struggle with life's darkened and cocooning stages. She writes about the challenge and necessity of learning to wait in the dark. Reading that book helped me make some sense of what I was going through, feeling discombobulated, and so lost in my own life and mind and spirit. I was able to rethink my wilderness experience as a time marked by God for my growth. As hard as it was, I seemed to be going through a necessary phase for new life. Reading that book reminded me that God can and, on occasion, does call us aside to the dark spaces, to the wilderness in order to teach us, transform us, and renew us. We can so easily forget that wilderness is part of the Christian journey. The world tells us that wilderness time is rarely meaningful, more a result of depression or dissatisfaction with our lives than an experience to value. But wilderness spaces can prepare us for inner transformation and new birth. I felt like God was showing me that my new birth was a process of transitioning from one life stage to another. By summertime I felt different than I had a year before—stronger, more self-aware and God-aware in a completely new way. Granted, this awareness came from times of deep pain and the loss of certain dreams and expectations. But now I saw those times of feeling lost and alone, unsure of my own identity, my own wants, my own future, as steps toward dying to an old sense of me.

All the while I also had been churning over what it means to be a

Christian, to be called to community, and to be part of the church. In a time when I felt I kept alone in my hermitage, when I didn't have the energy or desire to be in community of any sort, God began to stir in me these questions. Sorting through them was part of the rebirth and the new sense of self.

I was profoundly aware of God's presence with me, telling me to be patient and to recognize his presence. I sensed that God had not in fact forgotten me or abandoned me; rather, he was growing me, transforming me, and preparing me for a new chapter of my life. But I had to find the courage to let go of certain things in my life and to accept the call to move forward, to embrace a new part of me yet to be discovered, and to learn the things of which I was capable. I was already having labor pains.

Chapter 14

Companion God,
you gave Ruth to Naomi, and Elizabeth to Mary.
Surely you know our needs before we ask for them.

God must have slumber parties because some of the things God orchestrates in the Bible stories (like the timely pregnancies of Mary and Elizabeth) make me believe that God knows a thing or two about how essential girlfriends are to any kind of holy enterprise, whether it's praying, griping, imbibing, or birthing prophets and saviors. This brings me comfort because it means I'm not weird for imagining that some of my most sincere experiences of God are channeled through my gal pals.

I need to see a small handful of girlfriends regularly in order to keep breathing. I used to think "small handful" was a redundant phrase, but if I were a freakish giant instead of the petite blossoming six-foot flower that I am, my handful wouldn't be so small. So, it's all very apropos. Anyway, on somewhat of a consistent basis I find a way to see these women. They show up in their white lab coats and usually really cute shoes I undoubtedly covet, carrying steel briefcases with oxygen pumps and masks. And I am able to breathe for a little while longer. Nessa is one of those friends. When she and her husband left Durham and moved to San Francisco, I considered asking her to leave him and run away with me to Paris and then maybe one day we could all reunite on the Jerry Springer show. Deep down I know she would have thought about it.

I hate to admit it, but Nessa is one of those women I didn't like as soon as I laid eyes on her. She's long and pencil thin in an Audrey Hepburn kind of way, with a similar sense of style—classic and unassuming, and she always looks like she just blew in from a windy day, except *her* weather tousles her up just enough to be refreshingly beautiful and breathless. Most normal fallen women would not like Nessa upon first glance. But it gets worse. She happens to be fabulous: witty, insightful, and painfully perceptive, kind, gentle and full of love for anything with breath in it. Nessa also happens to be in the process of becoming an Episcopal priest. A former New York editor, she moved back home to the South to finish her seminary degree. She worked part-time as a chaplain's assistant and part-time as a pastoral intern at a small country church where the men say things like, "You sure preach good for a girl." So all those Sundays I was lying in bed skipping church, she was getting gussied up for another day as the priestly intern at Saint This Old Church or Another.

It is an odd blessing to be a church delinquent and have some of your closest friends preparing to commit their professional lives to the peculiar ways of God and God's people. The oddness of it is that you get to see genuine faith mirrored back to you, and sometimes it kind of resembles what you yourself understand about faith, that it comes and goes along a bumpy road of self-doubts, deep frustrations, and genuine bewilderment at how to reconcile the harshness of life with the adoration and praise of the holy. And there's a blessed beauty in such a reflection because it offers you hope that maybe if we're all in this together, together we can figure out a way to get each other farther along the bumpy road without losing sight of God. Together we can talk and cry and probe for God.

I remember when Nessa was trying to think her way through her first miscarriage and I was trying to feel my way through the end of my long-term relationship. We spent endless afternoons in her garden, she pulling and tugging at weeds and digging up ancient bulbs that never bloomed, and me trying to hold my balance in the hammock I was constantly flipping out of. One afternoon I watched her as she stomped about her dry garden, every movement a determined force to root out everything barren and lifeless. Her long matchstick legs sticking out of small baby-pink shorts, you know, one of those old, favored pieces of clothing from eighth grade that some folks, like Nessa, are still lucky enough to squeeze into. Her white, ribbed tank top was smudged with dirt, and long loose strands of thin wavy brown hair fell through the loose-fitting pink bandana tied carelessly around her head.

"I think I'm struggling with letting go of all the failures in my life," she blurts out, putting old oversized ski gloves over her tiny hands.

"What do you mean?" I ask.

"I've been having these strange dreams and they've got me think-ing," she says. "I mean, my body seems to know how to naturally get rid of its failures, right? So I'm thinking, why can't my mind do the same thing, instead of holding on to every darn mistake and screwup I've ever made in my life."

It takes me a minute to realize that we are now calling her miscarriage her "body's failures."

"I mean, why can't I let go of all the past failures in my life that keep me from being who God wants me to be?" she asks.

I cross my right leg over to the far left side of the hammock, shifting my weight as I turn to face her. I am wary of another fall. She has plopped a white footstool beside the hammock and is ripping out weeds from the clumpy earth in front of her. Her hands reach and grasp determinedly, pulling with a force that seems to ripple through her slight frame.

"Why don't you write it out?" I ask, offering the one therapeutic tool I'm familiar with.

"I can't seem to write right now. I just can't." Her voice is clipped and frustrated. "My friend Steph says it's because I'm in denial." She pro-nounces it "denaal," her Nashville accent pushing through like weeds through broken ground. "She says if I write it down, I'll have to admit it, and I don't want to admit it."

I'm not sure if we're talking about the miscarriage or other supposed failures.

"Well, maybe she's right. Once you write it down, it's real in a new way. But that's okay. Sometimes we're just not ready to admit certain things. When my father died, I stopped journaling for six months." My comments fall unnoticed to the ground like the clumps in her dirty gloves.

"Everyone in my ordination discernment group is into journaling and

writing down their thought processes." She moves her fingers dramatically back and forth in front of her face when she says this, as though suggesting a touchy-feely self-discipline she both covets and mocks. "I mean, should I be doing that?" she asks. "Should I be obsessing even more over how I can't believe God's called me to be a priest? How I can't figure out why God thinks that somehow I'm capable of this job? I can't even hold onto life he puts in me, let alone try to work through the fact that he thinks I can offer life as a priest."

It's a rhetorical question and she's not even looking at me. I don't know whether to encourage her or join in the pseudomocking.

"Would that somehow make me a more committed Christian or something?" she continues. Again, the note of questioning sarcasm.

"Why do you think you're holding on to your failures?" I switch the conversation back to what I know is buried under all this chatter. I have learned that the role of curious inquisitor is most helpful for certain people. It allows them room to seek after their own answers in the safety of friends.

"I don't know, because it's safer that way?" she replies. "At least I know who to be, how to define myself, and what feelings to expect. If I let go, what will be my story?" she asks. Before I have a chance to answer, she continues. "It's much easier holding onto our crippling stories than it is trying to narrate new ones. Isn't it?" She stops pulling weeds and holds up her dirt-caked gloved palm, a handful of tangled bulbs and roots and clumps of dirt. She looks up at me in the hammock, an expression of pained confusion mixed with defiant certainty.

"Definitely," I say. "Did you plant those last year?"

"No," she says matter-of-factly. "These are someone else's failures. How typical of me to be cleaning up someone else's mess."

The conversation, the circumstances seem almost orchestrated. I morph into my Shirley MacLaine inner goddess and smile at the universe, the beautiful, raw, painful honesty of creation journeying together. Before I can say anything, she throws a tiny root mounded only into the hammock

"Here you go," she says. She's dug up a stone about the size of an elongated quarter. I turn it around in my palm and see that carved into the rough surface is the word TRUST. This time I laugh out loud.

"You've got to be kidding me," I say. "Where the heck did this come from?"

Somehow Nessa misses the playful move. She replies without even looking up from the ground. "I just dug it up. Here's another one." She tosses another stone into my lap. This one says DREAM. The whole thing is ridiculous. I don't know what to say or do except to just keep turning the pebbles in my palm. Before she is through, Nessa throws three more stones at me, each one with a word carved into it: HOPE, BELIEVE, PRAY. Neither of us knows what to say, so we pretend like it's the most normal thing in the world to find these message-laden pebbles. "I guess the last person who owned this house buried them in her garden," she says.

All I can say back is, "Huh, interesting."

* * *

"I think one of the hardest parts of breaking up with Michael is that I really thought I was going to marry him." I am curled up on my therapist's couch, my legs tucked beneath me, staring at the books lining her shelf as I talk to her. I have this peculiar habit of staring off when I'm talking and trying to really think something through at the same time. I know she thinks I can't look her in the eye, but maybe she's getting used to my peculiarities by now. After all, it's our fourth session. She stares at me and I can't help thinking she's waiting for something more profound. But I know she's listening and waiting for me to figure out what I want to say next. I am getting used to her too. I've really gelled with this one. I love that she has a law degree and an M.Div. and spent ten years as an Episcopal priest before becoming a full-time therapist. I imagine I'm getting way more than my money's worth.

"And sometimes the thought that I might never get married and have a family is overwhelming. And I can't even believe I'm admitting this out loud."

107

"What's wrong with saying it out loud?" she asks.

I squirm a little in my seat and stare at the ceiling. "I don't know why I've always felt that admitting I really want a husband and family somehow might be like admitting that I wasn't the strong woman everyone thinks I am, like I'm supposed to be evolved beyond that need." I don't give her a chance to answer. "And I just want to know how to put that longing to rest. How do I do that?" I turn to look at her squarely in her eyes, "How do you put a longing to rest?"

"That's a really good question." We both adjust ourselves more comfortably into the ensuing silence. I learned a long time ago how comfortable I am with silence, and how comfortable I am with other people's discomfort with it.

"Why do you think you need to put your longing to rest?" she finally asks.

"Because it's really hard to live with. I feel like it's always on my mind on some level and I'm getting tired of praying about it. I feel stuck between the verse in Luke that talks about the nagging woman who bugged the judge so much that he gave her what she wanted, and the other verse in Matthew that says we shouldn't go on babbling like heathens in our prayers because God knows our needs." I lift both my hands in the air as if weighing the scales. "Am I the nagging woman, or am I the heathen?" I laugh, not really expecting an answer but just putting my confusion out there. She tilts her head to one side and looks at me sympathetically.

"It's tough, isn't it, knowing how to interpret the texts sometimes."

I tilt my head back onto the couch and sigh. "And I've got all these questions for God about it, but I . . ." My voice trails off.

"You what?" she probes. The silence is calming.

"I mean, maybe God doesn't want me to get married. Maybe I want a family so badly that if God gives me one I'll be so happy that God thinks I won't need him anymore. Isn't that stupid to think that?"

"I want to hear you say more about that. Do you think your longings are bad? Is it bad to desire a partner and a family?"

"No, of course not. But I have such a hard time imagining it's not totally selfish of me to be so consumed with it. Maybe God hasn't answered my prayers because it's not what God wants for me."

"What if you thought of your longing for marriage and family as a sign of it being a vocational call?"

"What do you mean?" I ask, sitting up straighter on the couch and leaning in toward her.

"Well, maybe instead of condemning your longings, you learn to embrace them differently. Maybe *reframing* is a better word. When we are called to something, we do all we can to open ourselves up to living into that call, but then there is also part of the call that requires us to be open to holy mystery and the divine process. Some parts of living into one's call are truly out of our hands and up to God how it will play out."

I immediately warmed to the idea of thinking of my desire for companionship as a call, but I wondered aloud how I could get myself to that point of reframing.

"How do I learn to reframe like that?"

"Just what you are doing now," she replied. "Talking about it and thinking on it."

As I sat in the quiet room taking this in, my therapist casually asked, "Enuma, what are your thoughts about sex?"

I looked up, a little uncertain. "Yes, please?" I laughed. "What do you mean?"

"Well, you've talked abut your desire for marriage and family, but what about sex? How do you process that desire?"

I liked this woman. She was a cut-to-the-chaser. Maybe every therapist-priest should have some lawyer in them.

"Well," I started cautiously, "are you asking me if I have sex, if I want sex. . . . What exactly?"

"I'm asking you more specifically how you think about your sexuality, especially in relation to your faith. And, yes, how you acknowledge and process your sexual desire is part of that."

I looked at the clock and noticed we only had five more minutes.

"I'm working through some of those questions, but I need more time to think about how to articulate my thoughts. Can we start out next time on this topic?"

"Of course, Enuma. I know we could spend weeks on some of those questions. I bring it up because I really want you to think about it."

She'd given me enough to chew on until our next session. I marveled at the notion that maybe God was calling me to marriage and it wasn't purely a selfish ambition or a means to have sex without the guilt.

Later, at home, I read the section on marriage in The Book of Common Prayer:

> The union of husband and wife in heart, body, and mind is
> intended by God for their mutual joy; for the help and comfort
> given one another in prosperity and adversity; and, when it is
> God's will, for the procreation of children and their nurture
> in the knowledge and love of the Lord. Therefore marriage is
> not to be entered into unadvisedly or lightly, but reverently,
> deliberately, and in accordance with the purposes for which it
> was instituted by God.

It helped to be reminded that I didn't create marriage; God did. But it was going to take some time to do all that reframing.

✷ ✷ ✷

"Bishop in the church of God, on behalf of the clergy and people of the diocese, we present to you Vanessa Lydia Martin to be ordained a deacon in Christ's holy Catholic church."

I am standing before the altar, behind Nessa and with the other three presenters. Nessa has asked me to be a part of her ordination ceremony. I can hear Fred, her two-month-old crying in the pews.

Has she been selected in accordance with the canons of this church? And do you believe her manner of life to be suitable to the exercise of this ministry?" the bishop asks. I want to say out loud, "By *manner of life* do you mean the way she takes care of her two little boys and supports her husband, following him around the country through medical school? Do you mean how she's gone through seminary in three different states, following her heart's deep desire to love and listen to the God who calls her to the priesthood even though she's scared shitless of not being worthy enough to baptize and serve Eucharist and care for the sick and the dying and proclaim people as husband and wife?"

But instead I join the others and say, "We certify to you that she has satisfied the requirements of the canons, and we believe her qualified for this order." I decide not to tell anyone that I have no idea what the "canons" are. I watch Nessa in her white alb, the only one of the three women being ordained who isn't wearing her ceinture around her waist, and whose hair looks like she simply ran her fingers through it after a shower and then stuck her head out the window of a fast-moving car. I smile, relieved that, even on the edge of the priesthood, she still exudes that slight wisp of disarray, a lover of God trying to keep her many ducks in a row just like the rest of us. God was getting another priest, this one with her diaper bag and her laundry list, and I believed the kingdom of God would be the better for it.

＊ ＊ ＊

The other day Nessa found her first free hour in days away from Fred and Tom, or "The Infant" and "The Toddler" as I like to call them. And she telephoned me. On her way to get a massage she called me and left me a message telling me she loved me, five times. I listened to her message five times and started breathing again. Sometimes God is in a hurry and has to get to the point. I bet Nessa was wearing really cute shoes.

Chapter 15

When I was in the fifth grade, my family moved to the Ivory Coast, and I walked into my new classroom at the International School sporting white shorts that should have been illegal and my favorite Michael Jackson tee shirt, the one with the picture from the *Thriller* album. I was fresh off the boat from America, and what was a carefully calculated wardrobe choice to win me new friends made me my first enemy, Liya. Apparently she thought I thought I was too cool for school and my Michael Jackson paraphernalia proved it. I, on the other hand, envied her familiarity with the school and my new classmates and her command of the French language. I've since told her that jealousy is a poison we drink hoping that the other person will die. Luckily neither of us died, and I learned how to make peanut butter and honey sandwiches in her parents' kitchen. We became lifelong friends and spent the next years of junior high more or less inseparable. Then we went away to our respective boarding schools, ended up at different colleges in the States, and continued our adult lives in different countries. Since finishing graduate school in international public health, Liya has lived in Costa Rica, England, Mali, Zimbabwe, Rwanda, and now Johannesburg, South Africa. Yet our friendship has never skipped a beat. I have boxes of old letters from high school days—when e-mail was nonexistent—and even letters from many of those foreign countries. Every now and then Liya and I meet up in New York and spend a few essential days together.

Liya knew me before I knew that Jesus knew me. She doesn't pretend to understand my faith or why I feel compelled to talk about God as

though he really were my Best Friend Forever. She just accepts that that is me. But she doesn't ask questions either, except for last summer when I was spewing off some sidewalk rage about people acting like the streets of New York were just an extension of their personal living space. Then Liya asked me laughingly, "What kind of Christian are you?"

She repeated her question a few nights later when I asked the bartender for my second *caipirinha*, a Brazilian drink made with rum, sugar, and lime. I told Liya I was an honest Christian and sucked the rum out of my complimentary sugar cane.

By *honest*, I mean that I can admit to myself, and to anyone who will listen, that I find it hard to be Christlike. I don't feel the urge to break out my pom-poms in complex cheers over the words *reconciliation*, *community*, and *self-denial*. Not because I don't want to be like Christ. I just really struggle with it. And every day of my life so far I am reminded that being a faithful Christian is a choice. Sometimes striving for the kingdom is a choice I make willingly, and other times obedience is like pulling teeth. But acknowledging I have a problem has proven to be a good first step in solving most problems. Of course I want to be perfect: to empty my purse at the feet of every homeless person I come across; to feel deep peace every time I agree to volunteer with a local mission project; to sit on the edge of my pew on Sunday mornings gratefully thinking there's no place else I'd rather be. I want to be the first in line when the roll call comes for giving up all my possessions and living amongst the poor. But that wouldn't be very honest of me, and I don't think it would make me a genuine Christian. I actually don't know any real Christians like that anyway. I am still trying to figure out what *would* make me a genuine Christian. It's not just about being good, but on some level don't most of us kind of expect compensation for our good behavior? When we realize there is no security blanket from life's trials, it shakes our world. What happens then? Faith becomes faith, and it's another opportunity to trade in our agenda and expectations for God's agenda and mystery.

I often wonder what the difference is between being a Christian and being a humanitarian. I should know the answer to this by now, and I do somewhat—the textbook answer. But how do the differences play out in daily life? Maybe I need to figure this out in order to remind myself why church is important, or really essential, to my growth. I am still just trying to understand community and what makes the community of believers so different from a bunch of really good-hearted people.

The distinction seems to be that in the church the focus is on God first, and second on who we are capable of being by God's grace. And with non-Christian humanitarians the focus is on people (or llamas and lemurs or the rainforest or other worthy foci). The church starts with God, and the Incarnation (God becoming human in the birth and life of Jesus Christ of Nazareth) keeps us focused on people and all creation in the long run because we are constantly reminded that God was once a human; God became a creature. And because we believe that everyone is made in the image of God, we strive to see God in everyone. Every day is a call to serve and love Christ in the people we encounter. Our instinct as Christians is to love as we have been loved, which includes loving all of creation and being good stewards of the earth. But because we start with God and end with God, that sort of love allows room for hope beyond ourselves and our actions. And because we believe that the church, the gathered community of disciples wherever they are found, has been given the Holy Spirit, we also believe that the Incarnation of God continues to manifest itself in creation.

* * *

On that same trip to New York I met another honest Christian. I was having dinner with a woman named Josie, a friend of a friend from back home. Josie is a free-spirited, accomplished artist. She's had shows all over the world but feels most at home in the heart of New York City where she lives. As soon as I met Josie, I could tell she was one of those people who see the world as though through a kaleidoscope: everything has the potential for beauty and light if seen through the right angle, and the broken pieces reflect the richest colors. After dinner we ambled along our

way, as much as one can amble on New York's sidewalks, back to her studio, stopping to pick up some small pastries, cookies, and coffee. As we got closer to the Port Authority bus station, I was keenly aware of less-cute coffee shops, and less-bright, bubbly couples and groups of people enjoying the summer evening. The groups of people we were now passing looked disheveled and without any set agenda for the evening.

As I took in my surroundings, Josie kept walking and talking as though she were an extra on the set for the movie *Pleasantville*—until we came upon the man lying by a Dumpster along the street. He looked like he'd fallen asleep in a drunken stupor and anywhere he woke up would be fine with him. One of his untied shoes had fallen off, and his too-small trousers barely covered his chapped dry ankles. Okay, remember when I told you that I was not like Jesus? I meant it. I shamefully admit that I would have kept walking past that man. I wanted to keep walking past that man. But as soon as she saw him, Josie stopped and immediately leaned over him as though she'd just chanced upon a little old lady who'd slipped on the sidewalk.

"Sir, are you okay?" she asked the limp figure, handing me her purse and bag of cookies.

"Look at him," she said to me without straightening herself up.

"Sir, can I get you anything?" She pushed some more.

I stood beside her, my coffee getting cold and my hands full of purses, and glancing around at whose attention we might be attracting. Josie got down on one knee and touched the man, turning him slightly so his face wasn't kissing the pavement. He mumbled drunkenly, clearly disoriented.

"It looks like you've had quite a rough time of things, huh?" she said to him.

I shifted my weight from one foot to the other. I could feel my discomfort rising and felt myself starting to get a little annoyed at Josie. What the heck was she doing? I wondered quietly. Clearly this homeless man was drunk, and standing here talking to him wasn't going to make a difference in his day or anyone else's. And how inconsiderate was it of how to do this during our short time together. This was the first time I'd met her and she didn't even seem to care how uncomfortable this whole experience was making me. I cringe now thinking back on my reaction.

"Well, why don't I at least help you put your shoes back on so you don't lose them? That would be an unfortunate thing to wake up to." She reached over to his lost shoe, picked up his dirty foot, and slipped it back into his sneaker. By now she was on both knees, sitting on her heels. She put his foot onto her lap and tied his laces. Then Josie saw his Walkman lying by his side and noticed his earplugs were falling out of his ears. She stuffed the plugs into one of his trouser pockets. The drunken man raised his head a little and looked at her, moaning incoherently. I wondered if he was as uncomfortable with this whole scene as I was.

"Sir, I'm going to leave you my bag of cookies. I'll put them right here under your jacket so no one takes them, okay?" She patted his leg and kept her hand rested there.

"I'm just going to say a little prayer for you, okay?"

Then Josie, right there in the middle of the city street, with people coming and going and staring at us, prayed for the man out loud. She asked Jesus to watch over him that evening and to help him get his life back to some sort of working order again. Then, as though she had done this a million times, she got up, wiped the dirt from her knees, took her purse from me, and started walking again. She jumped right back into the conversation where she'd left off, telling me how much she loved her neighborhood and how much she felt like the people around her were part of her extended family. She didn't say one word about what had just happened. Except for when we got back to the studio and were drinking tea on her couch. Out of the blue, she said, as though as an after thought, "Oh, shoot, I forgot to ask that man his name so I could keep praying for him."

* * *

When I think of church, I can't help but think about the idea of confession, of being part of a community where I can admit I'm not very good at

following Christ. And not just admit it generally but share some specific stories about where I've really missed the boat, like the Josie story. I guess that my hope would be that instead of judging me for admitting these things, the church would hold me accountable to repentance and to trying to be different. I don't have many friends who talk about things like confession and accountability. But it's something I bring up once in a while with a lot of my friends. I'd like to think of confession as just another way of speaking truth to one another, the kind of truth telling that can lead to grace and prayer and an ongoing recognition of our human tendency to slip up and fall into piles and piles of sin, the kind of sin wrapped around our seemingly mundane and habitual thoughts and ways of being. Then there's the other side of confession, the truth telling that seems a part of any faith community just by the actions of those who truly are faithful. Like Josie, whose actions admonished me simply by the reflection they held up to my own inaction.

✳ ✳ ✳

Whenever I have a revelation, I consider it my responsibility to share it with my friends—my Christian duty, if you will. So one Monday morning I walked boldly into Sophie's office, put my coffee cup down on her desk, and said, "I am a rich young ruler."

"Huh?" was her thoughtful response.

"I am ready to admit that I am the rich young ruler," I said, nodding my head to acknowledge my self-agreement.

"What are you talking about, Enuma?"

"You know the story in the Bible, where Jesus says . . ."

"Yeah, I know the story, but?" She lifted both her hands in the air, palms up like a clumsy yoga pose. "You don't have any money, and your worldly possessions ain't so worldly."

"I know, but if I had money, I wouldn't want to give it away. So that makes me the rich young ruler." She returned to her menial task of filling her printer and asked if we could continue this conversation later.

Sometimes I suspect that I am too complicated for my friends and they cannot process revelation in a timely manner.

But I meant what I said. I am the rich young ruler, and I don't want Jesus to ask me to give away my stuff. And because I don't want that to happen, I am patiently waiting for it to happen, for God to test my love by asking me to pack up my favorite pairs of shoes, my winter coats, and my purses and take them down to the Goodwill store off of Highway 54. Then the next step will be to start shopping at thrift stores and pretending I don't care what I look like when really I miss the comfort of my corduroy jeans and pair of well-worn Dansko clogs. There has to be another way to prove I love Jesus. But God calls us not to worry about things, stuff, and clothes. I struggle with that. Maybe he said that because back then people wore togas and sandals and he thought he might be doing people a favor by asking them to give those up. He had no idea about Memorial Day whites and summer dresses and what life would demand of my gender. It affects us worldwide.

I will never forget another revelation I had once while visiting my mother in North Africa. While walking through the local *sous* (market) in the center of Tunis, I had paused to pick through the colorful silk and cotton scarves at a vendor's stall. I noticed that two Muslim women at the next stall wearing *hijab*, the traditional religious headdress, were also picking through scarves, holding different ones up to their already covered heads and modeling for approval from one other. It was strangely reassuring to see that vanity knows no cultural or national boundaries.

Perhaps the "give away stuff" clause is just another way to strip us of our old identity, the part of me that thinks I really am what I wear or own or want. But I wonder why I am so easily smitten by pretty things and whether that is such an affront to God. Maybe it's not an affront to God but to other people who for whatever reason don't have access to the same pretty things. It kind of reminds me of what I loved about wearing uniforms all through high school. Everyone was made equal in that very basic way, at least for a time. Our personalities, talents, and flaws defined us more than our clothes. And there were fewer things by which to form

clear boundaries of who was "in" and who was "out." In a way we never lose that childish desire to figure out who's in and who's out and to try and ensure we are the former. But with God, the unfair thing is that everyone is in, no matter your previous history or fashion mishaps.

I also think God may actually appreciate beautiful things too. Of course, to some degree, my sense of beauty and God's sense of beauty might be somewhat mismatched, but God did give pretty clear instructions in Exodus about how his new digs should look. The tabernacle was going to be quite the hot spot—purple and blue yarns for tassels, fine linens and goat's silk, furniture with cherubs made of gold, fragrant oils and spices to scent up the joint. Yes, I am left to surmise that God might also watch the Home and Garden Television Network. I have also surmised that I'm still learning how not to put God in boxes.

Seriously though, would it be so awful if the church were more of a place where we seek beauty and try to understand what beauty is through the capacities God has given us and in the Spirit's ongoing revelation? Isn't it an old theological and philosophical tenet that beauty is bound to goodness and truth and inextricably linked to the things of the spirit and the nature of God? I don't have all the answers, but I'm happy to pose the hard questions.

Part Three

Hope Has Walls

Chapter 16

Miracle-working God,
help my unbelief.

I've been reading the Bible again, trying to find where it says church is supposed to be interesting. I really believe that the apostle Peter started an interesting church but most of the churches I have been to have been boring with a capital *B*. Very little has challenged or compelled me to be any different than who I was before I walked into the sanctuary. I have heard plenty of good sermons that make me think or muse the way I would after a really good lecture or story. I have also heard sermons that make me feel guilty about being who I am, a middle-class American citizen with health care, a private education, and endless choices of sugared cereal in aisle 6. But I can't remember the last time I heard a sermon that threatened me with endless grace, no matter my circumstances, no matter my actions, while at the same time reminding me that God calls me to be so much more than I am. I imagine that kind of news would bring the tourists and make them want to stay a while.

A few weeks ago I was talking to my good friend Henry, whom I've known for years. It was a Saturday night and before I hung up he invited me to visit his church the following day. Henry is a pastor who has been commissioned to start a United Methodist church plant in a growing community. I told Henry to e-mail me directions and I would definitely be at his church the next morning if I could haul my ass out of bed. But I also told him not to hold his breath or take it personally. The next morning I happened to wake up in time to feel guilt-ridden enough to support our friendship by going to the service, even though I didn't feel like it in

the slightest. I walked into the community center the church rented on Sundays and sat down in the last row, closest to the gym exit. I wasn't planning to stick around past the Eucharist. And then my friend got up to preach the sermon. Before he was finished, he told us that God was throwing a party and he dared us to come, to walk boldly into the kingdom of God.

I wish I could offer you a less cheesy narrative of what happened next. But the cheese is about to ooze. Maybe it was seeing Henry up there in his pretty priestly vestments that his awesome wife, Holly, had sewed for him. Maybe it was because the girl sitting next to me looked about my age and had such a warm and welcoming smile. Maybe it was just because one of the greeters was really cute. Whatever the means, the end was that I felt something shift within me during that service, and like a crazy fool I wanted to go to that party God was throwing. Even though I already knew what the party was about and would probably show up at the door with a beer in one hand and wearing the Been There, Done That tee shirt, I was foolishly curious all over again. Yes, I wanted to go to the party. Something small and quickening inside me wanted to know if things could be different because standing up there speaking to us, my friend Henry no longer looked like just old Henry whom I'd known for years. He looked like someone who really believed in God's event-planning skills. Actually, he kind of looked like he'd been to the party, and he was here to tell us that *stuff was going down.* I wanted to know what kind of stuff could go down and if any of it would be going down here, at this church. And that's about all I knew after that first service.

* * *

I only just found out that John and Charles Wesley, the founders of Methodism, started a Bible study group in college and that was how this whole thing began. The group met regularly and never got bigger than twenty-seven people. Other students made fun of them for how they were so into learning about the faith and trying to be disciplined believers. Folks called them "The Holy Club" the same way we might say "Bible bashers" today. The young men had all sorts of rules for their little get together: they had to read the Bible; have regular devotional time with God; actually do things for other people like feed the hungry, visit the sick and those in prison; and they had to ask themselves a series of questions every day that forced them to think about their daily choices, thoughts, and actions. As impressive as all that is, that's not what gets me. What gets me in a "praise God, there's still hope for me" kind of way is that John Wesley didn't even consider himself a genuine Christian until years after this holy club had disbanded! All the do-gooding, scripture-reading, community-building, devotion-taking attempts at being church does not a man of faith make until these practices are done out of sincere faith in the triune God and heartfelt belief in the ongoing redemptive work of Christ in one's life and in the larger world. It would seem that doing whatever it takes to make oneself open to such a place of faith is the initial and necessary discipline. Even if it takes leaving church for a while and then tiptoeing in through the back door.

✳ ✳ ✳

When I stop to think about what I believe, I find my faith has the shape of an amoeba, but not so much shapeless as constantly shifting, finding the most appropriate form to encounter the changing world around me. It has taken me a while to be okay with that, to find comfort and hope in a faith without rigid lines and sharp angles that stab more than define. Many things about Christlike Christianity aren't so open to fluidity and shape-shifting—aspects, or truths even, that we need as the solid base of a faith that grows and stretches and contorts itself to exist in a broken world. I know the creeds are mixed into the mortar of that base, and I have to trust the church and the communion of saints to help me understand that base, especially when life's circumstances goad me to start my amoeba dance.

Perhaps I should begin each day by reading the Apostles' Creed, to remind myself about the basic outline of what I believe and hope in, what

I more or less kind of stake my life on, at least theoretically. The creed is a nice succinct springboard from which to jump into the daily pool of decisions and reflections I find myself swimming through on a regular basis. Yes, some parts of the pool reach the depths of death and despair, but most often, thank God, I'm paddling around issues like shopping, relationships, and how to keep the Mosaic law—otherwise known as the Ten Commandments—especially the one about coveting, oh and the one about idols, and ummm . . . sabbath. If I lived with a real awareness of the creed as a general template for daily life, things might look different. For example, when I'm at the cash register whipping out my credit card to buy yet another black turtleneck, I can do a quiet check to see where that fits into my belief cheat sheet, my creedal outline. *Extra black turtleneck—let's see: "creator of heaven and earth . . ."—nope; ummm, "born of the Virgin Mary . . ."—nope; oh, maybe somewhere before "will come again to judge the living and the dead."* Okay, I know it's not that easy (nor is it really about black turtlenecks), but there is a lot to be said for thinking through what we do believe about the faith and about what makes the church the body of Christ.

Creeds are as good a place to start as any. After all, they are what we believe, the symbols of our faith. They are a big part of what we're supposed to learn about in church while we're slowly trying to wrap our minds around the crazy story we hear on Sundays. For a long time I thought that story started with Jesus born in a stable. Actually I didn't really have a clue how it ended or even what came before the cross incident. I didn't grow up going to Sunday school. I grew up reading the children's Bible by myself, sprawled out on the living room floor, trying to make my own connections between the cartoon drawings of little lambs and little Zacchaeus with the frightening crucified Christ suspended from the cathedral ceilings. No one told me there was a sequence to the Bible stories, that Moses and Jesus weren't playmates but lived in different historical periods, that the Israelites who crossed through the wilderness were related to the Christ who hung on the tree, and that actually we Gentiles were the new kids on the block when it came to sitting at God's Table.

What I did learn I picked up on my own, the way I picked up old Coca-Cola bottle caps for my childhood collection of instant treasures. Up until college my creed would have gone something like this: "I believe in God because 'they' told me to. I believe God made heaven and earth because it sounds like just the amazing kind of thing a God should be able to do. I believe in Jesus, but I'm not sure how he's different from God the Father. I believe I've heard of the Holy Spirit, but he kind of sounds like a third wheel to me. I believe I'm supposed to go to church because that's what people who believe in God do."

Things have changed a little with my seminary degree and all, but I really want to think that I could have gained some of this insight without a master's degree. What I want to believe is that the church could have clued me in a little better. As an adult I have found myself gratefully amazed at the pastors and teachers who somehow manage to convey sound teaching to those of us squirming for knowledge and understanding about the faith and about God's commitment to humanity.

Chapter 17

Nourishing God,
you offer yourself as a banquet for our hungers.
Help me to savor your goodness yet never be
satisfied.

I went back to Henry's church the following Sunday. And this time he said that the church was a construction site.

"What do you need to build a church?" one of the pastors asked the group of squirming children. An interesting question, and I was eager for the little kids to offer their suggestions to the pastor. The children's sermon can be a great way to get some sound theology.

"A cross!" One kid shouted.

"A table!!"

"Important things!"

There were some budding theologians in the mix. The student pastor acknowledged their responses and moved on to the real lesson he wanted them to learn. "I am going to teach you a song called 'I Am the Church' because that's what we really need to build a church—people. God has given us all the materials to build God's church."

This brief exchange presented much to work with. I found myself frantically jotting down notes on the back of the bulletin. Yes, God has given us all we need to build the church but there sure was a lot to unpack in the one-word answers from those kids. A cross is not a bad place to start when we think about the church. Maybe if we learned more about the role of the Cross in the Christian journey, we would be less taken aback when life doesn't turn out the way we imagine or God doesn't come out of the magic lamp after we've rubbed our palms numb. A cross reminds me that God became man out of a love I cannot measure and then God defeated

death and stepped off the cross, defying the rules of nature. And a cross reminds me that no matter how bad things get or how down on myself I can be or how many times I fail to measure up to whatever or whomever is measuring me up, I am still on the path to wholeness, being made one with the deep and vibrant richness of God and always only steps away from holy love in any direction I falter. If the cross is part of the foundation for building church then the church becomes a place where celebration is due and thanks is given and I can look around and see that I'm not the only one whom is loved with such an incomprehensible love.

There's something else about a cross that helps me understand what makes a church. The crosses I grew up with were crucifixes, with the image of Christ dying on the beams. There is a difference between an empty cross and a cross on which the Son of Man is impaled. Each takes you down a slightly different road and prepares you a little differently for the journey. The crucifixes of my childhood offered me an unmistakable object lesson: deep love comes at a great cost. And while the love of God did not cost me all that it could have because of the grace of Christ, it still comes at a cost. Freedom is not cheap. In God's economy freedom from sin and death is an exchange for binding oneself to what is holy. But here's the trouble. What is holy and of God does not come naturally to those of us who are familiar with and comfortable with sin and death.

The cost of traveling with the Divine is enduring lifelong ceremonies of minideaths of self. No matter how rich and vibrant the journey with God, the death of self is difficult and painful. If you're taking the Christian invitation seriously, these little deaths can and should happen in all areas of your life because the love of Christ seeks to invade all areas of your life—from your home to the workplace, to school, to the grocery store, to the gas station, to the nightclubs, to the battlefields, and to the pews. Nowhere is safe from costly grace. So for the romantics out there (of which I am one, unfortunately) who want to slip their hands into the bloodied palm of Christ and skip through fields of lilies singing songs about how sweet it is to be loved by Jesus, I have a horrible news flash. Your lover is scarred; there is torn flesh and there are gaping holes and the fields are full of sinners. But there *is* good news, even if it doesn't always sound like good news. If all those sinners are willing to embrace and follow a scarred and servant Savior, then the field becomes the church, and the canvas of love is stretched out beyond the sweet (and sometimes saccharine) to include sacrifice, obedience, and an increasing willingness to become the scarred body of Christ for an aching world.

I don't mean to say simply that suffering is part of the Christian journey. What I'm getting at is that building the church has to include teaching people about expectations: God the Father had expectations of Jesus, and Jesus has expectations of us, and all those expectations—the feel-good ones and the challenging-as-hell ones—are all wrapped up in a larger story, a story that started long before any of us could say, "Crawl into my heart, baby Jesus, and make it your playpen." So the Cross is not a bad place to start at all.

∗ ∗ ∗

But I can't tell a lie. I'm really, umm, glad? thankful? thrilled beyond words? that we don't have to stay at the Cross *all the time*. Now that would suck. I have to give a shout-out to the kid who yelled that we also need a table as a necessary foundation for building a church. He had no idea how much we need that table, the place where God promises to meet us every single time we step forward to receive the bread and the cup. In all the months I spent away from church over the years, I never stopped missing the Eucharist. The bread and wine are another way that Christ remains incarnate among us, made flesh still in the here and now. I wish I could string together random beads of words to illustrate what it means to me to take Communion. Each time I walk up the aisle to the Communion servers, I always feel like I am walking up to meet Christ. And there's a weird mixture of awkward embarrassment, longing, joy, relief, and anxious impatience swirling around my insides. I feel terribly unworthy, greedily hungry, and deeply grateful all at once. If I had my way, I would stand there in front of the Communion servers and have them each feed me the entire loaf of bread and the whole cupful of wine, one piece and one dip at a time as they boldly assured me over and over again that the body of Christ was broken for me and the blood of Christ was shed for me. When I am up there at that Table I feel like I fully understand those lines in William Blake's poem "Auguries of Innocence" that go: "Hold infinity in the palm of your hand, / And eternity in an hour." The world as I know it seems unbounded by time, and everything that matters seems layered into that small piece of bread soaked in wine. You could get me to say yes to pretty much anything in those few seconds it takes for all this to go down. Because for those brief eternal moments I truly believe that all things are possible.

Yet, when I happen to be on the other side of the Eucharist, when I happen to be one of the Communion servers for the day, the experience differs entirely. It's not just about me and Christ in those moments; it's about Christ and everyone else, and it's an amazing gift to get to see that from the vantage point of the one bearing the cup and holding the bread. Being a Communion server is the only time I ever feel like a superhero, and my special ability is deeper vision. God somehow enables me to see all those to whom I offer the bread or wine in a way I never see them otherwise: they actually look like people I could love. They actually appear a little innocent and childishly yearning for God. And I actually feel humbled and honored to be the one getting to spoon-feed them the body of Jesus Christ in manageable bites. But as soon as I put the elements back on the altar and return to the pews, I lose my powers. In no time at all I am already back to thinking how annoying David is when he makes that noise in the back pew, or how I can't believe Melanie wore that outfit to church. It is shamefully and gracefully true that we are all sinners struggling to be lovers of God in this space between kingdoms. I think that every person who goes to church should take the chance to offer the Body and Blood of Christ to everyone else in the church community. The change in perspective is gift upon gift.

I cling to the fact that God promises to show up in certain places. As much as it delights me that God can be playful and full of surprises, showing God's self in the least expected situations, I am equally thrilled that specific places exist where, whether I believe it or not, God can always be found. The eucharistic Table is one of those places, where God says, "Enuma, no matter what you've got going on, no matter how busy you might think I am, no matter how deeply you've given up on me, I *promise* if you come to the Communion Table, I'll meet you there and we'll give this all another go." So I go to the Table and I find that the Table is connected to real people's hands and those hands are connected to faces and even where I'm expecting God to show up, God still surprises me by showing up in ways I hadn't imagined. Yes, most significantly in the bread and the cup but also in the people who hold the bread, who extend the cup, who sing the songs as I feast on Christ, and whom I pass in the pews as I return to my seat. God reminds me that God can be in all those places and people at once. I am starting to wonder if part of the miracle of going to church, even when I'm terribly dissatisfied with most of what goes on in certain churches, even when the church has no walls and meets in a gym, is that God will still show up there because God has promised to do so. The church will always be poked through with human sin, and some churches will do a worse job than others, but that doesn't change the miracle of Christ choosing to wed himself to the church. She is still the bride of Christ, sullied and all. And I have to believe God takes the "for better for worse, for richer for poorer, in sickness and in health" stuff pretty seriously.

Chapter 18

Beckoning God,
you call us at the most inopportune times,
when we're set in our ways and terrified of change.
Equip me to turn and repent and follow you.

Two months into attending Henry's church I met someone who unintentionally made me realize that maybe I was part of the problem with the church. Maybe I had gotten so used to the "facts" that I couldn't see the miracle of it all. I met this man in the midst of doing a very "un-Enuma" like thing one night.

I went to a public place where I didn't know many people and stood in the drizzling rain, hymnal in hand, singing out loud and passionately about wanting some "figgy pudding," wanting it "right now," and not leaving until I "got some." Granted, I also sang about a town called Bethlehem and encouraged folks to deck their halls with boughs of holly. It was my first official time caroling, and if the church hadn't promised a Christmas party afterward, I'm not sure I would have signed up. But I'm glad I did because I met a man there named Joel, and while we were standing in the drizzle waiting for the rest of the brave few to join us, we talked, and he mumbled something about needing atonement and having had a past full of deep wickedness. Suddenly I was willing to yell for figgy pudding if it meant we could keep talking. Mainly because I'd never met anyone who so humbly, sincerely, and casually said something like that in getting-to-know-you conversation. When Joel said the word *atonement,* I heard an honest desire for confession and forgiveness. (I was also grateful that I had gone to seminary, because otherwise I would have suggested he try the Macy's cologne department.) When he said *deep wickedness,* I sensed it was related to systemic violence and

skewed vision. So of course I asked just as casually, "What kind of deep wickedness?" and I learned that Joel had been in the army many years ago. After having seen and done the things he did in the army, he was haunted by questions and deep regret. I also learned that Joel had been an English major in college and loved to write. I told him that now we had something else in common besides needing atonement and knowing deep wickedness and suggested we continue talking later because the troops had gathered and it was time to go a-caroling. Only I didn't use the word *troops* with him.

When we got to the Christmas party, Joel and I had a chance to talk more over some holiday beers and treats. He told me that this was his first time ever really going to church in the past fifty years or so. It was a big step for him to be in a sanctuary. For the most part he had been an atheist and had spent most of his adult life in the army. Joel told me that he saw a lot of unmentionable things in the army and took part in many of them. But then his eyes were opened and slowly he came to see that he was on the wrong side of the fence. He had a conversion of sorts and became extremely involved in speaking out against war, with political and social activism—writing columns for local newspapers, publishing books, and protesting when necessary. Joel was intense. To lighten the mood a little (after all it *was* a Christmas party), I asked what he thought of church as a newbie. He said he felt like he was forming a community outside his family and the people from work, and these people really seemed to care about him without even really knowing him and all he'd done with his life. I almost told him that it was really hard to believe that he'd done horrible, unmentionable things in his life because he had the kindest eyes I'd seen in a long time. But I just listened as he talked some more. He said he had a lot of questions and it was hard trying to become a Christian. He leaned in closer to me and said, "I've got to talk to the pastor because I've been wondering about this whole baptism thing, how will I know when I'm ready. It seems like a big deal to me, not something to do lightly. I kind of think about when my grandson was born and I experienced both intense joy and terrible fear, because I suddenly realized that I could love someone so much that my life was going to get much more terrifying."

I told him he had pretty much hit the nail on the head: becoming a Christian would probably make his life more terrifying. And I knew he knew about terrifying experiences. But I also told him that the terror sort of goes undetected for a while and then it hits you just when you think you've got the whole thing down. That's usually when God calls you to something more, something more challenging and demanding and ultimately life-giving. I told him that one of the cool things about baptism, besides eternal life with God and ultimate salvation, is that you're not baptized into the faith to go at it alone; you are baptized into a people who are supposed to walk with you and go through the terror and the joy alongside you. "You have to learn to walk with them as well, through their terrors, joys, and callings." And I told him the walk is filled with so much grace it is almost unbearable.

The thing I probably should have told Joel that night was that if he ever decided to be baptized into the church, he would have to remember that ultimately he didn't choose Christ; Christ chose him. And being a part of the church requires constantly learning what that means—to be chosen and invited into a new way of life, a life flowing out the triune relationship of a Father who creates, a Son who saves, and a Spirit who sanctifies, makes us holy. We each have to figure out the dance between living into our unique identity as an individual created by God and our identity as part of an eternal community of saints. The church plays a role in guiding us to discern our particular gifts and in calling us out to use them. But instead of saying all that to Joel, I simply said, yeah, he should talk to the pastor, but God would also let him know when it was the right time to take the bath.

Joel e-mailed me the next day and called me a mensch. I wasn't sure if I was willing to let that slide, but then I looked it up in the dictionary, found out it was a good thing, and peace was restored to the land.

✳ ✳ ✳

The other day I was driving in the car with Sophie and David, her six-year-old son. David is fabulous. On more than one occasion he's been known to stare, transfixed, into his mother's eyes and tell her that he sees Jesus there. Luckily, Sophie does not assume this might get her a free ticket through the pearly gates. I think she needs to put more coins in the Salvation Army bucket at Christmastime. On more than one occasion I have stared into her eyes and told her so. But I digress. On this particular car trip, David had some health tips for us.

"Mom," he piped. "Here is a list of things that are really good for you: dancing, music, laughing, and dribbling."

"You're right, David, those things really are good for you," Sophie said. "But dribbling?" she asked. "You mean like when you dribble a basketball?"

The sound of exasperation in David's voice was classic. "No, No," he sighed. "There's three different kinds of dribbling! One, when you dribble a basketball. Two, when the weather is bad and it's dribbling outside. Three, when you're running and you don't go too fast or too slow. That's called dribbling."

I listened intently to see where this conversation was going.

"Oh, you mean like when we ran that race yesterday and I told you to pace yourself?" Sophie asked.

"Yeah," David said. "That's called dribbling and it's good for you."

Sophie had told me how she and David had run a one-mile family fun race the day before.

"Hey, David," I chimed in before Sophie could question her child's etymology skills. "Do you think you could remember that list so when we get back to your house I could write it down? That is an *awesome* list of things that are good for you."

"Sure, but I don't understand why you need to write it down." He said it as though only a weirdo without a brain wouldn't remember such an easy and obvious list of good health tips.

"I know, kiddo. I can't believe I have to write it down either. But just remember it for me, okay?"

"Sure, Nu-Nu," he replied.

I think I'm going to practice dribbling at church. I'm really, really liking the service and the people, and it actually seems like God hangs out there. But I want to take it slow, pace myself through these initial laps. Yes, dribbling is definitely called for. I'll have to pass this tactic on to Joel.

Chapter 19

Intimate God,
you walked with Adam and befriended Moses.
Give me the courage to nag you relentlessly
as a holy lover.

I'm taking the next step. I've decided to get more involved in this new church so I started going to a midweek Bible study called Theology on Tap. A couple of guys meet at Killian's Pub on Tuesday nights, and over some pints of Guinness we talk about things like prayer and faithfulness. For a while I was the only girl and it was great. My presence seemed to bring out some latent chivalry in the men that made them do things like walk me to my car and buy my beer. I knew I had a good thing going. But then I guess word got out that Enuma had sort of scored with free beer from some sweet Christian guys, and the women started flocking to *my* Bible study. I am usually hospitable, but now the guys don't buy my beer any more, and I've considered leaving the group until they really miss my amazingly insightful contributions and start saying things like, "Hey, Enuma, we miss you on Tuesdays. You should come back. We'll even buy your beer." Then I will know it is the season for more growth.

During one of our first meetings someone raised the question of whether or not we could ever nag God. How long should we keep praying when our prayers seem to go unanswered? Of course the textbook answer is keep praying until you get an answer but also pray to recognize the answer when it comes. That's easier said than done. It is terribly hard, for me at least, to be persistent in prayer. When I pray, I want answers in at least a month. But rarely does it happen according to our own time lines. Why is that? Would it be so hard for God to just get right back to us and let us know yay, nay, or maybe say? It seems God could resolve a lot of human

frustration and pain if God answered our prayers right away. But then there's that freakin' catch about how we're not always ready for the things we pray for, nor do we always pray for the things that are best for us. Both of which are frustrating. And I should clarify here. I'm not talking about praying for world peace and the ease of natural disasters, for the end of hunger. Those issues are bound to take more than a month to resolve. I'm talking about smaller-scale prayers for guidance and discernment, and of course my wish for the perfect mate, which actually could lead to world peace because if he's as perfect as I'm hoping, he'll eventually change the world and make it a better place, while still fixing me pancakes in bed on Saturday mornings. See how smoothly it could all work out?

But on a serious note, I don't think we can ever nag God. Nagging suggests we're being a pain in God's proverbial ass. Bringing our cares and desires and worries to God is never a pain in God's ass. Maybe God experiences holy frustration when we can't seem to see the answers God's already provided, or when we refuse to redirect our prayers as the Spirit guides us. But overall I'm choosing to believe God would rather be in ongoing conversation with us about whatever plagues, haunts, or disturbs us than have us pretend we're so divinely patient and willing to ask once and trust that if it's meant to be, it will be. When I look to the Bible, I don't see any of that saccharine shit going on. I see Hannah on her knees wailing at God. I see Sarah who's so impatient she takes matters into her own hands and gets her husband to impregnate Hagar. I see Abraham pushing his luck and asking just one more time for God's mercy: "Okay God, what if there are *ten* innocent people in Sodom and Gomorrah?" I see a widow harassing a judge day and night until he finally gives into her just to shut her up. I see Jesus telling his disciples to ask, seek, and knock—three active verbs that require more than a momentary effort. Come to think of it, it's kind of awesome that we serve a God who wants us to articulate our thoughts, to argue, to be persistent, to not give up easily, to go ahead and make our mistakes and learn from them. That's good parenting, isn't it?

It's sort of a win-win situation when you think about it. We are free to bring our hearts before God, and God is free to grant us our desires, redirect our desires, or convict us of our desires. The key point being that it's ultimately not just about us and our individual pleas and prayers. God's got a bigger picture that we graciously get to play into. The fact that we can argue with God and plead with God and offer repetitive suggestions to God maybe means that God's open to our being a little in on what God's up to. Henry preached once about how God is a God of vulnerability and improvisation. I interpret that to mean God doesn't necessarily know the play-by-play of how everything is going to work out. The details are kind of left up to us because God's chosen to give us free will. What God *does* know is that everything will work out somehow. That's God's promise. There isn't a paint-by-number plan; there's a living God who dreams and desires just like we do. But God's dreams and desires are purely good and for the well-being of all creation. It's difficult to remember that sometimes.

* * *

I bit the bullet and signed up for the new-members class at church.

It doesn't by any means mean I am committing to the church. It just means I'm committed to think about joining a church. Henry said the class would be a refresher on what Methodism is and what it means to be a Christian. It sounded safe enough. I went to the first class and there was no Kool-Aid in sight. I figured I could come back. All was going well until we were asked to take a spiritual gifts inventory. Apparently there are twenty gifts listed in Paul's letters in the New Testament. Everyone is gifted in some way by the Spirit in order to help nurture and expand God's kingdom. I started getting worried as I read the list of discerning questions I found on the United Methodist Church Web site. They were brutally to the point and I knew I had to be brutally honest in my answers.

I see what God is doing in the world and explain it to others.
   I put a star in the "seldom" box.

I don't mind doing what needs to be done, no matter how small or seemingly insignificant the task.

I put a star in the "seldom" box.

When someone asks for my assistance, I gladly help without thinking about what I would rather do.

Hmmm, "seldom."

I scoured the list and finally found something for which I could check "most of the time":

Delegating responsibility comes naturally for me.

My answers to the sixty questions looked like a connect-the-dots picture of a pilgrim walking down a well-intentioned cobbled road to hell. I don't like serving other people. I don't look for opportunities to share my faith. And I do not offer as much time and money as I can to further God's work.

But that's not the point.

The point is that I've chanced upon a church that actually believes it's important to help people figure out how God has gifted them and where they might need to use their gifts. To me, this translates to a church that actually expects something back from me and will not be content to let me slip in and out without making me really think about what I have to bring to the ecclesial table and in effect to the wider community beyond the church walls. Could it be that a faithful church has a responsibility to help people discern what God might expect them to do with what God has given them?

Learning about spiritual gifts reminds me that God equips God's children to come together and live into God's dreams and desires for the world. Part of the ongoing process of locating myself in God's ever-blossoming kingdom includes being active in a church community that tells me again and again that a sacred story defines who I am and what I should be doing with my life and with the gifts of God. Often that story

144

will come into conflict with who I already think I am and what I already assume I should be doing with my life. Because other endless loud and extremely convincing narratives about *consumption, feeling good, personal identity,* and *nurturing self* easily draw me in but have little to do with *community, radical hospitality, obedience, discipline, worship,* and *the kingdom of God.* Perhaps the bonus gift is that I am also learning that Christlike community takes shape within regular old relationships. Nurturing such relationships helps me better hear the central story.

Chapter 20

Healing God,
have mercy upon us.

Remember what I said about God loving slumber parties? I have more evidence to back up my theory. But first I am going to add to my theory what I believe is the indisputable fact that female friendship is the secret to making it through life and actually contemplating doing it all over again if the choice were an option. If the afterlife does not include close girl-friends, then heaven can wait. Now, back to the growing evidence. I have met some amazing women at this church—women who look like they could be on the cover of any magazine by the checkout aisle at the grocery store. Well, not *any* magazine. It would be weird to see them on the *National Enquirer*. None of them have two heads or gave birth to centaurs. They are amazing mostly because they have no idea how beautiful they are, especially on the inside where it really counts. Though if I had to be honest, I'd probably choose being really gorgeous over being really nice. I know that's shallow and most of you reading this are probably passing judgment on me right now. That makes me sad. Does anyone have a mirror to help me lift my spirits?

Still, inner beauty notwithstanding, that's not even what I like about these women the most. What I like about them the most is that they believe life is worth laughing about to the point of tears. Even when it's hard to distinguish whether the tears are from joy or pain.

In the short time that I've known these women, it's become apparent that no matter who you are or what you look like or what you do for a living, life will provide each of us plenty of opportunities to make crazy

cocktails of tears and laughter and drink them down as both prayers for help and toasts for courage.

It is fair and accurate to say that these growing friendships are teaching me more about what it means to be the church. I am learning bits and pieces about how to take care of others and to allow myself to be taken care of with humility, vulnerability, accountability, and confession. It makes me think of the biblical stories of healing a little differently. That perhaps there is an aspect of healing that is simply the result of being in the presence of Christ, a way in which our souls are mended when we show up before God, open and honest about the particular ways in which we are broken in body, mind, and spirit. I guess I am suggesting that the mere presence of God is itself part of what makes us a little more whole. And the more I interact with these women (okay, and the men too) outside of Sunday morning church the more I get a truer sense of what the church looks like. Somehow the act of walking through the liturgy together on Sunday morning makes us more pliable the rest of the week, more flexible with the shape our interactions take, and more open to showing up just as we are—cracks, fissures, duct tape, and all. Because we are learning to recognize the Christ in one another, we are also more susceptible to being healed just by being in one another's broken yet holy presence.

* * *

I'm trying to get better about how frequently I log onto e-mail, to stop checking it as though I work for the CIA and constantly expect life-altering messages that must be decoded and attended to immediately and discreetly. It's hard to break the habit, especially now that I'm registered on Facebook. There really *could* be life-altering messages waiting for me on my profile page. What if I got tagged or winked at or asked to join a cause? The "Women in Support of Freeing Junior High Girls from Their Love of Dolphins" might need me to sign up *now*. So, for the sake of the tweens and to the chagrin of dolphin jewel smiths worldwide, I'm still pretty much checking my e-mail every half hour.

TINK! A message!

Hi, Girls.

Claire will be going to Sloan Kettering Hospital in New York on Monday to inquire about chemotherapy treatments. This is last minute, but is anyone free tomorrow morning for coffee and prayer? Just let me know a convenient time and place if you will be able to join us.

Love, Anne

You know how some people resemble certain types of animals? Some people remind me of birds or lizards or horses. Claire is one of the few people I know who reminds me of a flower. She looks like an English Rose. Not the petals and thorns but whatever you imagine when you hear someone described as an English Rose—exquisite, breathtaking, soft, feminine, Victorian, and yes, even silky to the touch. She has milky skin, cheeks always looking freshly flushed, and thick brown hair. When she walks, you can tell that she used to be a dancer—ballet of course—the only suitable dance for an English Rose. Claire is a doctor at one of the finest hospitals in the nation, and she has two young children for whom she cares with her ex-husband.

I met Claire for lunch about a month ago at P.F. Chang's, where I crave their orange ginger shrimp and brown sticky rice. After we'd ordered, I asked her how things were going. An easy question to which I expected an easy, off-the-cuff answer.

"I've been thinking a lot about what we talked about at your house at the last book club."

"What, about how much irrational fear affects our decisions?" I asked.

"Yeah, but more so the part about trying to figure out if the difficult things we go through in life are God's way of teaching us lessons."

"And what are you thinking?" I prodded.

"Well, I'm thinking that I totally do not agree with what Renee said. I don't think everything happens for a reason. I think sometimes really crappy stuff just happens because we live in a broken, messed-up world."

I could tell there was a personal stake in this.

"Did you talk to Renee about it?"

"Yeah, we talked on the phone. I know that's how she's narrated life's circumstances most of her life and how she wants to explain away why she can't get pregnant. But I can't see life as so black and white. I don't think God had me marry Steve and deal with all that emotional turmoil and stress and then get divorced and break my children's hearts just so I could learn some life lesson! And I definitely don't think God is making Renee infertile just for character development."

"I kind of agree," I said. "Some of the shit that happens in life is because all of creation is broken. I also think that half the time God is just as crushed and hurt as we are when shit happens."

"I just wish Renee would give herself some grace," Claire said.

"I think so much of our embedded theologies are residual from how we learned to see the world growing up and our roles in our families," I offered. "I know I'm still dealing with my crap from childhood. There are so many voices that go into making us who we are and unfortunately not all of them are helpful."

We let the conversation trail off, but I could see Claire was still preoccupied.

"What else is going on with you? How's work?" I asked.

"It's fine. I was so tempted to call in sick today, but I couldn't justify it to myself because I feel fine physically."

"A mental health day is just as important as a physical sick day, Claire."

"I know. It's probably good that I stay busy." Her voice trailed off and she tried awkwardly to change the subject. "Enough about me. I'm here talking your ear off. What's up with you?" The water welling up in the corner of her eyes told me that I hadn't quite heard enough about her.

"What's up, Claire?" I asked firmly.

She looked down at her hands resting on the table. "Well, I guess I don't have fibroids."

I wasn't sitting on the brown rug. "What do you mean?" I asked. "The surgery didn't get rid of them?"

150

"It turns out they weren't fibroids. I spoke to my doctor on Monday."
She looked back down at the table, her voice softer than usual.

"So what is it?"

"We're not completely sure, but they think it's epithelioid leiomyosarcoma.

"What's that?"

"Well, they found a tumor the size of a grapefruit in my ovaries."

I touched her hand, looking confused and not completely sure what all the medical jargon was hiding. "Claire?"

She looked up at me with her doey brown eyes.

"Are you trying to tell me you have cancer?" I finally asked.

"Yes."

The waiter showed up with my orange ginger shrimp.

* * *

I listened as Claire shared and vented and asked unanswerable questions. Right when she thought her life was getting back in order after her painful divorce, her difficult move to a new area, and her earlier battle with what she thought were fibroids, this happens. She wondered aloud why God would bring her to this seemingly new and hopeful space in life, where she'd finally found a church and people she was growing to care about and trust and where she felt like life had new possibilities, only to let her get cancer. And now she had to make the phone call to schedule a hysterectomy. The first step on what could be a long road of surgery and chemotherapy. I tried as gently as I could to do some reframing—maybe God was graciously involved in the fact that she'd reached a new place of hope and church community. As unbearable as this new diagnosis is now, there are more people to walk with her. When we left the restaurant, I asked Claire if she would be weirded out by me praying with her before we left. She said that might be the best part of her day.

The night before Claire went into surgery, six of us women—Renee, Anne, Sarah, Lauren, Holly, and I—went over to her house, made tea and cookies, sat on her living room floor, and basically just hung out. I passed my jasmine green tea bag around and made everyone smell it because, as I told them, I wanted them to know what the country of Tunisia smelled like, at least the parts I'd been to. Then we talked about the navy doctor guy who was pursuing Claire at work and how he'd just invited her to a weekend BBQ with his *friends*. Which of course meant he wanted them to check her out and give the thumbs-up or down. And which of course meant that she had to consider very seriously what she would be wearing to this sham of a BBQ. We considered taking a field trip to her closet and suggested that she go with pretty but casual—maybe a nice sundress with flip flops to dress it down. Eventually, as is to be expected, the conversation turned to female wax jobs and how hard it is to get insurance to pay for breast reductions. Lauren openly shared her latest waxing experience. On a foolish whim she'd decided to go all out and get a Brazilian wax job—you know, where they take *everything* off. She and her husband were going on vacation and she figured what the heck. Well, the heck turned out to be one of the most painful experiences of her young life (no, she doesn't have children.) The end result was a cleanly shaven, menacing pirate who snarled at her husband for a good twenty-four hours when he couldn't understand what the big deal was.

When we were full of sugar cookies and the appropriate tea had been spilt on the rug, Claire brought up the "gold star" complex.

"So you know how whenever people go through really painful illnesses and then die, everyone always says how brave and strong they were to endure it all, and it's like they get a gold star for putting up with the tragedy of it all?"

We nodded and mumbled recognition.

"Well," she continued, "I was lying in bed last night and thinking about everything that could happen in the coming weeks and months and. . . ." Her voice broke and she choked back tears. "And, I already feel like such a failure because, you guys, I can't even be brave enough to get the stupid gold star." She dropped her head and started openly crying.

I reached out and placed my hands on her thighs, and Annie rubbed her back.

"I'm scared and I'm not brave. I don't want my hair to fall out or my skin to peel off. I don't want to pump my body with poison to try and kill this thing that's eating me up inside. But I have to do whatever it takes because of my children. I have to."

We sat quietly around Claire, listening and weeping with her as she confessed that if she didn't have any kids, she would just wait the cancer out and live her life because she feels that at thirty-three years old, she's already done so much living for which she is deeply grateful. In the midst of our weeping we started to pray, and we asked God for miracles and courage, for healing and hope, and for Claire's hair, if it does fall out, to grow back really curly and maybe even red. And I secretly thanked God for making Claire's gold star shine so brightly among us.

Chapter 21

The first call came as I was getting ready to meet an old friend for dinner. Michael, my ex-boyfriend, hadn't shown up for work that day and no one could get hold of him. The second call came twenty minutes later as I was walking out the front door. One of Michael's roommates had finally come home, opened the door, and found Michael in bed, just as he'd been the night before. He had not woken up this particular day.

When Michael died, my brain lost its ability to function for about seventy-two hours. I found my way to his house in less than ten minutes. I made the phone calls—to his best friend in LA, to all our friends, to his new girlfriend of seven months in Boston. I sat outside his house that night for five hours giving policemen contact numbers for his parents, making them reassure me over and over again that they would let me know as soon as officers in New Mexico had been dispatched to his parents' house bearing the unbearable news. I waited for his mother to call me. I waited for the coroners to come. I waited for someone to tell me this was not really happening. I waited for someone to show up in a white lab coat and fashionable dress shoes with a tank of oxygen so I could perhaps start to breathe again. My girlfriends started coming that night.

* * *

Nora later confessed that she didn't know what to expect as she drove the three hundred miles to be with me. She had been through grief with me before, and she knew my response was up for grabs. When my father died five years before, she said there was a space I wouldn't let anyone penetrate, and she had felt helpless as my friend. So when Michael died and she called me to ask if she should jump in the car and head my way, she couldn't believe I actually said yes. Especially since she had just spoken to Sophie, who told her that she, Sophie, had come to my house late that night of Michael's death and I wouldn't let her in. Sophie had sat vigil outside my front door while I curled up in a ball and wailed on the other side.

But Nora came and she had countless cups of tea with me, and she let me cry, and she made all my flight arrangements to the funeral in New Mexico, and she went with me to meet Sarah, Michael's new girlfriend. Sarah had just flown in from Boston, and Michael's mother had asked me to please travel with her to New Mexico because she was in too much of a state to travel the distance by herself. Nora was there when I walked into the living room of the home where Sarah was staying. I instinctively reacted to Sarah's bawling at the sight of me by rushing to her side where she lay on the fold-out couch. I cradled her head in my lap. Nora was there as I whispered my certainty of God's promises to Sarah, to be present in the midst of death and uncontrollable grief. Nora was there when I later confessed through tears that I knew Michael was experiencing more peace now than he ever had on this earth and that I knew he would never trade that to come back here. And Nora was there to go to church with me on Sunday, four days after Michael's death, when I wanted so desperately to be surrounded by the people who were slowly becoming my new family and by the liturgy that proclaimed God's peace and offered God's body and God's blood to uphold the weary. Nora was there when I was too physically weak to get to church by myself and too scared to walk to the Communion Table without someone behind me to catch me if I fell apart with grief.

* * *

In Michael's childhood bedroom in New Mexico, I had a few moments to myself. I lay on the bed and started to journal.

I wonder what you would say to me now? We used to run out of words and sometimes we said too much. I saw that you kept everything I ever said to you, even the Post-it notes and quick scribbles. Jason found the box with my name on it and gave it to me. I started by reading the thank-you card I sent you after our very first date, five years ago. In it I wrote, "I could have talked with you for hours." And the next four years were spent trying to figure out how to live into so many of the words we used to say, "I love you."

I figured out one more way yesterday. I boarded a plane with your new girlfriend and helped her fly across the country to see you for the last time. I kept my hand on her lap, I wrapped her shaking body in my arms, I made jokes about people mistaking us for a progressive lesbian couple and somehow I bet I ended up being the man. She told me you would find that funny. She told me a lot of things I already knew about you, but I listened like a new friend, nodding and smiling and exclaiming with each new anecdote about your seven months together. She told me you were about to propose to her and that you had looked at rings. I didn't know that because whenever I had asked you awkwardly each time we talked if you were engaged, you always told me you were never even close to that. You always had the strangest sense of taking care of me, always well-intended but usually slightly off. I have to admit I sort of like her. Maybe you two might have been happy together. It's hard to tell after only seven months.

She said she knew so little about our time together, and I didn't have the heart to tell her much. I just told her that I knew you at a different time and that we loved one another differently than what she had shared with you. I let her craft the stories she needed to make your time together "pure" and "destined." Maybe it was. I can give you the benefit of the doubt. We made it to your parents' home after a full day of flying. By then I had

already gotten used to taking care of her, kind of how I got used to caring for you so quickly.

I've been trying to figure out how I feel about your being gone. It's almost like a part of me has died too—that part that you brought to life for me. You were the love of my life in so many intimate ways and now you no longer exist. It's hard to imagine where you do exist now. I've never lost someone so intimate before. What does it mean for what we experienced together, all those words I wrote you that have now come back to me, sitting by my bedside in a large white envelope? But I know you're here, Michael. You woke me up the night I prayed that you would make yourself known to me somehow. I forgot to tell you I love you. I know you never questioned that, but I'll say it again anyway. I love you. Always.

I revised the Apostles' Creed two weeks after Michael died unexpectedly in his sleep. In the new version I kept everything the church fathers had agreed upon and added only parts I thought were fitting, the parts appropriate to add two weeks after death sneaks in and slugs you below the belt leaving you reeling in disbelief at the blow. This is the updated version. I have no scheduled trips to Ephesus or Nicaea, and no appointments with any emperors or bishops that I can recall. Hence, I am assuming that there will be no councils to refute this creed, so you might want to go ahead and commit it to memory.

I believe in God, the Father Almighty, creator of heaven and earth.

I believe there are spaces where heaven and earth collide and the things of this world are not as bereft of God as they may seem, where angels fumble over one another, bearing our burdens back to God and God's mercy back to us.

I believe in Jesus Christ, his only Son, our Lord.

I believe in a Savior who knows deeply of sorrow, of emotional abandonment, of carrying other people's crosses, of asking God if God is indeed present at the time of death.

He was conceived by the Holy Spirit and born of the virgin Mary.

I believe in the Spirit's power to invade the body of Christ, the church, and bring forth life when we, as a body, might feel too inexperienced to bear such a birth.

He suffered under Pontius Pilate, was crucified, died, and was buried.

I believe there are those of us who are tempted to wash our hands of things we do not understand, who would rather step back from the drama of being in the midst of God's work, in the midst of human tragedy and divine suffering. But I also believe that those parts of ourselves are called to crucifixion, to death, and to burial with Christ.

He descended into hell.

Even God has been to hell.

On the third day he rose again.

I believe in the resurrection of the dead—mind and body and spirit. I believe that those who can't accept new life even in this life do not fully understand the miracle of Easter. I believe we all have some degree of the "doubting Thomas" gene. But even Thomas got to see . . .

He ascended into heaven, and is seated at the right hand of the Father.

In the Incarnation we see God wrapping God's self in human frailty. In the Ascension all that is human is subsumed into the trinitarian community so that just as we are never bereft of God, God has chosen never to be bereft of our frail humanity.

He will come again to judge the living and the dead.

I believe that God's judgment will surprise most of us, that those who have condemned themselves might discover how much time they wasted.

I believe that God's judgment is found on the cross and the last word is mercy.

I believe in the Holy Spirit,

I believe that we are never left alone or expected to walk the path of faith without divine assistance and intervention, that God names God's self comforter, teacher, counselor because God knows the heart of men and women,

the holy catholic church,

I believe God is doing a new thing in all crevices and corners of creation, that no single church can claim to contain the fullness of God, but rather we—as members of Christ's body—are called to learn together what it means to be a creature. I believe this is a hard lesson to learn because we spend so much of our lives acting as though we are Creators.

the communion of saints,

I believe in the witness and faith of those who have gone before us, who are with us now, as fellow broken pilgrims together doing our best to mourn together, rejoice together, imagine together, worship together, and eventually rise together.

the forgiveness of sins,

even those sins of which we struggle to forgive ourselves and of which we are incapable of forgiving others.

the resurrection of the body,

because life in Christ has implications for our flesh as well as our spirit, because we are not called to spiritualize the faith but to live into it in this earthly world amidst the beauty and the mess that earthly living brings.

and the life everlasting.

That life begins now, calling us to live in such a way that when the fullness of God's kingdom comes we might recognize ourselves as able citizens of such a world.

Amen.

I've started talking about Michael. But it's hard. My therapist wants me to learn to tell the story again, of my life with Michael and my life now that Michael has died. I like the idea of it, of being able to re-live some of those memories with someone completely new, someone who didn't know him and doesn't even really know me but wants to listen to me tell the story. But I am afraid of the barrel of tears that might burst open inside me and drown the Enuma who is learning to cope. But I've started telling my therapist the story because there are beautiful and transformative parts of the story that continue to feed me, and to keep him alive.

Knowing Michael expanded my ability to love and to know compassion, and to embrace both the joy and tragedy of life. That sounds cheesy, but it's true. In the weeks following Michael's death, while arrangements were being made on what to do with all his things, I went to his house, into his bedroom and took the framed illustration of him sitting in the wheelbarrow that he had kept on his wall. I came home, and with tears

in my eyes, I hammered a nail into my own bedroom wall directly facing my bed and hung the picture so I'd see it every morning when I wake up. I know now that there's room in that wheelbarrow for two, and in my mind's eye I have etched myself beside him; God is pushing me along the tightrope too. I suspect that wheelbarrow is going to keep growing in my imagination, and I will start etching more people in there, both the living and the dead, because God has to care for all of us.

I can't help thinking that how I process Michael's death—or my relationship with him—has everything to do with my spiritual walk. Working through this experience is part and parcel of learning to understand that there is so much I cannot understand. I have to figure out what kind of peace I will make with this ongoing revelation and how it will affect the way I open my heart in future relationships and in the peculiar one I have with God. How we live into the daily mundane relationships in our lives says so much about how we imagine God and God's relationship to us. Our daily lives say tons about our embedded theologies, what we believe in our heart of hearts about God and goodness and life.

Chapter 22

I have decided to cleanse my colon. I read somewhere that a toxic colon can cause fatigue, headaches, high blood pressure, and digestive problems. I have these problems. My doctor told me that stress and grief can cause these symptoms too. I am saddened to say that I also have stress and grief. But at least I am in therapy for that. A clean colon can mean invigorated life and a body cleared up to receive all the nutrients it needs to function optimally. I told Sophie about my mission to colon cleanse and how I read that when John Wayne died, he gave his body to science and science found forty pounds of fecal buildup in his colon. We decided that from now on whenever we think someone is full of shit, we would simply say they are totally Johnwayned. We also decided that such a euphemism is more educational in nature than disrespectful to the dead. Some people really need to clean up their shit. In any case, I am going to drink lots of detox tea, internal parasite killer, and colon cleansing herbs. And I know that all my problems will be solved in three to six weeks. Which of course is comforting.

* * *

"I think God wants me to detox my heart." I was talking to Sophie on the phone late Saturday morning.

"What do you mean?" she said in between yelling at David to stop dipping his finger in his little sister's juice and trying to clean up the kitchen.

"Well, I finally took some time to listen to God. I feel like he's been whispering things to me for about two weeks now. And this morning I decided to just listen. I feel like I'm always rushing around doing errands or cleaning the house or trying to keep up with both work and my writing projects. I can't remember the last time I sat still and read and listened and journaled and prayed."

"Uh-huh. David, do you want a time out?" "I'm sorry, Enuma. I'm listening."

"It was almost like God was telling me to give my heart muscle a rest, like it's been overworked lately."

"Well, let's see. In the past six months you've started a new job, Michael died, you took care of his girlfriend and flew her across the country to be with his family, you joined a new church and are more committed than you've ever been in your adult life, and you're trying to finish a book due in three months."

"I know, right?"

"And in the last five years, you lost your father, left your job with no savings to freelance for a year, had an intense three-and-a-half-year relationship with a recovering and relapsing alcoholic, broke up, spent the past year getting over each other, finally started to figure that out, and—I hate to mention this again—but he dies suddenly and you take care of his new girlfriend."

I hate it when Sophie plays local historian of my life.

"I gotta go, Enuma. David and Anna are out of control this morning, and Jim is out running. Can we continue this later?"

"Sure. Call me later."

* * *

I know it sounded obvious—giving my heart a rest. But it hit me like divine revelation. Somehow it felt like affirmation that God was and had been present throughout some of those really shitty times. It sort of overwhelmed me to think that God knew my heart was tired and needed a rest. It's such an intimate thing to recognize and know about someone. The detox part really was like a lightbulb, because as soon as I quieted myself enough to listen to God, I knew right away what that meant—putting my romantic relationship with Michael to rest for good. Even though we had been broken up for almost two years when he died and he had already started seeing someone, we had stayed close friends. That made it virtually impossible to let go completely of the history of us.

Now my mourning his death was getting all wrapped up in reliving some of that history, even aching for some of that history. It was different than just reminiscing about the "good ole days." It was more about subconsciously holding on to a gift whose blessed time had come and gone. It seemed God was asking me to open up some much needed storage space in my heart for the new gifts that might come. Gifts that included a stronger, clearer sense of self and the ability to better name the aspects of healthy relationship I needed, whether in the form of a life partner or my growing sense of community. Yet at the same time, I experienced a deep affirmation of my need to grieve the loss of Michael, his untimely death, and how the world really is different without him in it. The flip side of all this heart detox and rest was that God was also inviting me to trust God in a deeper way with my worries, fears, and longings.

Chapter 23

Lord, of heaven and earth. . . .

The night that Claire called I was getting ready for bed around 11:00 PM. I knew something was wrong.

"It's happening," she whimpered.

"What? What, Claire?"

"My hair. Tufts in my hand."

"I'm coming over right now, okay? I'll be right there."

I hung up the phone and dialed Sarah's number. Her husband, Jon, picked up.

"Hey, Jon, sorry to call so late. Can I talk to Sarah, please? It's really important."

"Is everything okay?" he asked.

"Yeah, just get Sarah."

"Hey, Enuma, what's up?" Sarah asked.

"Claire just called me and her hair has started falling out, and she's freaking. I don't think she should be alone tonight. I'm heading over there now. Do you want to come with me?"

"Oh my gosh, Enuma, of course."

"Okay, I'll come pick you up."

By the time Sarah and I got to Claire's house, it was close to midnight. When she opened the front door, her eyes were red and swollen and she held wads of tissue in her hands.

"Oh, guys, thanks so much for coming. I feel so bad for freaking out and calling. I knew this was going to happen," she said.

We brushed off her apologies and hugged her tight. Then we went straight to the kitchen and put some water on the stove for tea.

"When did it start?"

"This evening. I took my sweatshirt off and all this hair came with it. So I ran my fingers through my hair and look . . ." She showed us strands that came loose when she combed her fingers through her thick beautiful hair.

"Oh, Claire," was all either of us could manage.

We moved into the living room with our tea and sat on the floor.

"I think I'm going to just go get it chopped off tomorrow before the kids get here."

"Have you looked at wigs yet?"

"No, I haven't been able to bring myself to do that. But I guess I have to now."

"Are you sure you want to cut it off, Claire?"

"There's no way I am letting my kids see this," she said quietly. "I guess I have to call the hairdresser in the morning. But even then I just can't bear the thought of sitting in that chair and watching her chop it all off."

We were all quiet.

Sarah and I looked at each other.

"Well," I started hesitantly, "we could do it tonight if you want."

"I cut Jon's hair all the time." Sarah said.

Claire looked up with wide eyes. "Really? Are you serious? You would do that?"

"If you want us to, Claire, we will."

A look of stubborn defiance came into her brown eyes. "Damn it, let's do it. I'm gonna control this part. If it's gonna fall out, I'm gonna control when it happens!"

She got up, placed her hands on her hips, and looked at us daringly. "Come on then."

Sarah and I looked at each other one more time, uncertain what we'd started but somehow as sure about this as Claire was. If she was going to lose her hair, we would be by her side in whatever way we could. We followed her to the bathroom and laid down towels around the sink. Claire handed me the scissors and gave Sarah the razor. Neither one of us wanted to take the first cut. I gave the scissors to Claire.

"Here. You have to make the first cut, Claire."

We all looked at our reflections in the bathroom mirror as Claire raised her hand to the middle of her head, lifted up a huge chunk of hair and chopped it off like she was taking charge of a pesky problem.

"There. Let's do it," she said.

"How much do you want off?" Sarah asked

"All of it." There was no question in Claire's reply.

A slow, mischievous smile crept onto Sarah's face. "So you want to do anything fun while we're at it? Any hairstyles you've been dying to try?"

"Yeah, like a mohawk or a mullet maybe?" I added, grinning.

"What the heck, let's do it all, girls. We can take pictures, and I'll send them to Henry. That should give him a good laugh at the church office," Claire said.

The air was heavy with the weight of what we were doing and humor lifted things a little. I couldn't help feeling a little bit of awe and gratitude that I was able to share in this moment with Claire, that I was able to share this with Sarah. We had all met at church just over a year ago—Annie and her twin sister, Holly, Lauren, Renee, Claire, Sarah, and me—and we had spent the past fourteen months fostering unbelievably deep and nurturing friendships.

Sarah and I took turns cutting chunks of hair off, fashioning Claire's mohawk and mullet. Claire stopped us at one point and ran to get her camera. We posed for pictures, extending our arms to get self-portraits of the three of us, laughing hysterically at our bad barber techniques.

It wasn't until Sarah started the razor that the laughing subsided. We looked again at our reflections in the mirror: Claire sitting on the stool, Sarah and I hovering over her, her head patchy with chopped-up hair, the chunks all over the floor, the strands all over the sink, the razor buzzing

in Sarah's hand. That was when the weeping started—three pairs of eyes suddenly brimming with tears, lips biting, hands reaching for tissues. We shaved Claire's entire head bald that night in her bathroom. Later, I described that midnight shaving to Henry as holy ground. It felt sacred and ordinary all at once.

Chapter 24

Living God,
Surely you raise the living as well as the dead.

It's been sixteen months since Michael died. Now I only think about him a few times a week instead of every day. The grief is easier because it does not feel caught in my throat like it did before. But in a strange sense it is also more difficult because the reality of it has burrowed underneath my skin and is always with me. Now that a year has passed, it is difficult to accept that from here on I will say things like, "This time last year Michael was not alive," or, "Michael would be turning thirty this year."

I am different than I was sixteen months ago. My internal life and my external life have characteristics that Michael would not recognize. I have moved homes. I have developed new friendships and new crushes. I am rooted in a church community. Even though it has all been good growth, it makes me sad to imagine that Michael will never know these parts of my life.

On the anniversary of his death I wrote Michael a letter. I tried to name the peculiar ways I was still sorting through the piles in my heart, trying to figure out what to keep and what to bury in regard to my love for him, my knowledge of him, and the history of us. I asked him if somehow he could help me in this second year learn even more ways to say my good-byes. I buried the letter in my backyard on Easter Sunday underneath an Easter lily.

Chapter 25

Magnificent God,
all honor and glory is yours, now and forever.
Amen.

These days I listen to the words during worship more closely.

"Feed on him in your hearts, by faith, with thanksgiving."

"Lift up your hearts."

"We lift them up to the Lord."

"Let us give thanks to the Lord our God."

"It is right to give him thanks and praise."

The liturgy is starting to sustain me. I am beginning to hunger for it by midweek. And now when I have to be out of town on a Sunday morning, I find myself always aware of when it's 10:30 back home, the time service begins. I find myself thinking of the people I would normally be sitting beside. I find myself feeling a little off-kilter because I am away from the church that seems to have become my home.

The liturgy reminds me why church might actually be important after all. It is where I am forced to remember my baptismal identity, my eternal calling and my role in this family of saints and sinners. Each week that my sins are forgiven I get to start again. Just when I thought it was "game over," God says, "Take, eat; this is my body which is given for you. . . . Drink this, all of you; this is my blood of the new covenant which is shed for you and for many for the forgiveness of sins. Do this . . . in the remembrance of me." I didn't choose Christ; Christ chose me. I'm open to learning what that means. Jesus was an amazing student of life and had a keen ear for poetic metaphor and a vibrant imaginative capacity. I hope my new church will teach me to be a good student, to crave learning and to seek wisdom and clarity in imaginative ways. And for my part, I'll keep showing up at worship because God promises to meet me there. I'm slowly accepting that God's presence is not always based on feelings. Just like my love of God, which cannot always be based on feelings. Loving God requires practice and routine just like love in human relationships. I need to remember that *I'm* the human in this particular relationship.

* * *

Two years have passed since I found a home at All Saints United Methodist Church. I wish I could say it was perfect, that having a home church has made me want for nothing more. Gosh, more than that, I wish I could say that one day I walked into the gym where our church gathers and there sitting in the middle row on a fold-out metal chair, saving a seat for me with his hymnal, was my godly man with great hair and partially achieved life goals. But that wouldn't be true. What would be true is for me to admit what I have found in regard to men: the ones who go to church are just as broken and oftentimes as disappointing as the ones who don't. I'm sad to say I have also learned that good hair does not always make for the perfect man. "Gasp, shock, horror." But again, I digress. I was talking about how church hasn't baked life into an apple pie.

My longings are still as deep as before, but honestly they feel less weighty. Part of what I am learning about my church community is that when you share the Body and Blood of Christ with people on a regular basis, you start to figure out that it's okay to share other parts of your life with them as well—the joyful, hopeful parts and the dark, suffocating parts too. I am learning to share my life more openly and to walk more boldly into the lives of others.

* * *

"So what are you doing for your birthday this year? Throwing yourself another party?" Sarah and I had signed up to be greeters together that

Sunday. We stood behind the table in the makeshift narthex waiting for the first churchgoers to arrive.

"Actually, yes, I am. But this time I want to have a ladies' brunch with just our group of girls," I said.

"That sounds fun. We can all bring something. But why not a big party?"

"I don't know. I'm turning thirty-six, and it's been a long year. I want to surround myself with my girlfriends and celebrate the beauty and tenacity of women in general."

"It sounds great, Enuma. I'm there."

* * *

I had decided to host the brunch on Valentine's Day, a week after my actual birthday. I had told everyone to be prepared for a surprise. As I set the table and got ready for my birthday celebration, I felt full of gratitude for the women in my life and I hoped they would humor my surprise activity. My girlfriends came one by one that morning, bearing gifts and food and coincidently all dressed in varied shades of pink. We mixed our champagne and orange juice and ate more carbs than any of us needed. And then I made a request.

"Since we're all here this morning, I was wondering if we could do something special."

"Is this the surprise?" Annie asked eagerly.

"Not yet. That's after brunch. But this might get you in the mood. I was wondering if we would each take a moment and think about one area of our life and maybe share with one another what we hope and long for this year. It seems like we never give ourselves enough open space and permission to dream and hope boldly and aloud with one another. It's like somehow we don't think that's an okay thing to do. So I want to do that today with you all, on my birthday."

The women around the table got quietly reflective.

"Gosh, that's beautiful Enuma. But also kind of hard," Annie said.

"I'll start," Sarah offered. "You all know that I'm trying to figure out the next step vocationally in my life. It's been really hard, and some of you have listened to me cry and get impatient and frustrated. I guess I hope that this year I'll get a clear picture of how God wants me to use my gifts and my education in the areas I am passionate about. I want to find a job that blends my love of people and different cultures and social justice."

One by one, each woman shared her hopes and dreams for the coming year. Annie wanted to grow more fully into her relationship with her boyfriend, Max, and to discern whether the long-distance was worth it. Claire wanted to get her body back to something she recognized and delighted in. After six months of inexplicably difficult chemo treatments, her cancer was in full remission.

Renee wanted to find peace with her seven-year inability to conceive a child and to start imagining other faithful and fulfilling ways that she and her husband could welcome children into their lives. She could not quite give up her longing to be a mother, but she knew she had to stop trying to find reasons why God might want her barren.

Lauren shared her hope that her life would stay as full and healthy as it had in the past year. She admitted feeling guilty about how well things seemed to be going in her life, and she often feared that her luck was about to run out because eventually it had to, didn't it?

Holly hoped she could find more faithful and healthy ways to draw clearer boundaries in her life—both professionally and in personal relationships. She was getting tired of trying to be everything to everyone. She felt that she needed to learn more than ever how to stop and take time to remember what she wanted on a daily basis and in more long-term capacities.

And me—I hoped I could live more fully into a new year, that I could find the courage to expect good things in regard to the state of my heart, my mourning losses, my longing for companionship, and my hope for renewed joy.

After we shared our hopes, we held hands around the table and spontaneously offered up prayers for the many things we had mentioned. Each woman prayed openly and boldly for another woman at the table, and the tears began to flow as freely as the mimosas.

"Okay, lady. The surprise better be less emotionally draining than that," Claire piped up.

"It is! It's going to be fun! Are you all ready? Drumroll please. . . . *We're making collages!!*"

"Huh?"

"We're making collages," I repeated. "I got everything we need and it's all set up in the other room. We're going to take some time to make posters of our hopes, dreams, and longings. I even cut the backboard paper so each collage can fit into a 16 X 24 frame. There are no limitations or filters with this, guys. We'll use the magazines and create a collage of images and words that speak to the things we just shared around the table."

"Oooo, that sounds fun. I can't remember the last time I made a collage! Let's go already," Annie said. Her beautiful smile and infectious spirit were always so contagious.

We moved into the other room and spent the next hour and a half working on our collages, laughing and eating little treats, even though we'd just finished a rich brunch. As each woman completed her collage, she showed it and explained the different images and words she'd cut from the magazines and glued to her board. Every collage truly seemed to capture the spirit and longing of each individual creator. Renee ran out of space on her board filled with nursery rooms, family rooms, and children's clothing, plus images of calm waters, books, and places that suggested peace and rest. It was a gift in itself just to see Renee be so lavish in naming her desires. A week after my birthday brunch, Renee went on vacation with her husband and they conceived. She is now five months pregnant with her first child.

* * *

I know life doesn't always work out easily and that our prayers are not always answered in recognizable ways. I know that making collages does not put an end to cancer or infertility or even to relationship and vocational concerns. I know all these things. Solidly. But I also know that healing takes many forms. Sometimes the parts of our hearts, minds, spirits, and bodies that receive healing can look nothing like the healing for which we've prayed. And therein lies the risk, not so much that our prayers fall on deaf divine ears but that we might miss the measure of healing we end up being given.

The women with whom I sat around that table are part of the foundation of what I experience as church. Knowing and being known by them is just one more piece of the healing I am slowly learning to live into as the days and weeks continue. It is a healing that mends my own spirit, mind, and heart into spaces where I can both more easily receive and more easily offer grace, humility, peace, trust, and joy. It is a healing infused with scents of God.

Epilogue

You tell us, Lord, that some shall see visions
and others shall dream dreams.
Give us courage to share our visions and our
dreams with one another.
Amen.

During my first Advent at All Saints I felt called to share my love of writing with my church community. I began writing weekly reflections to help us tiptoe into the new church year together as a church family. The response was so positive that I felt compelled to continue the weekly devotions as one way of using my gifts and passions to serve. Nearing the one-year mark of when I began attending the church, I had a peculiar dream and wrote the following reflection.

* * *

Ho, everyone who thirsts, come to the waters; and you that have no money, come, buy and eat! Come, buy wine and milk without money and without price.—**Isaiah 55:1**

I woke up this morning dreaming of the Eucharist.

The body of Christ broken for you. The blood of Christ shed for you.

Over and over I heard these words coming from my own mouth until they woke me up, and I realized where I was, in my bed, slumbering from sleep at 6:15 in the morning. I had been dreaming of church—our little gymnasium with the makeshift altar and the table for bread and wine.

In my dream I was asked to serve Communion, and I watched people come down the aisle—the little kids first as usual. It was the sound of the church proclaiming the gift of reconciliation that woke me up. And for a few minutes all I could do was lie in the dark repeating the words in my head, unable to shut it off: "The body of Christ broken for you. The blood of Christ shed for you. The body of Christ broken for you. The blood of Christ shed for you." I lay in bed asking God what he wanted me to get from this dream, and that's when I realized I had to turn on the light, climb out of bed, go to my computer, and just start writing—for me and to you.

Something has shifted. I do not regularly dream of sacraments and of people feeding on Christ. It has been even longer since I dared to dream of a church community. But here you are, a channel of God's grace, sneaking into my sleep and my spirit, speaking the only words that could ever sum up the extent of God's love and the endless call to come and be made whole again, if only for a moment. And in the past year so many of us have hungered to be made whole again and it seems there have been many moments. Some have been specifically mine, some specifically for each of you. But the bread and the cup we've shared suggest that these moments have been true for all the saints.

In the midst of the sudden death of loved ones, friends, lovers, children, you said, "Come and eat. This is the body of Christ broken for you and the blood of Christ shed for you."

In the joy of new births and baptisms you said, "Come and eat. This is the body of Christ broken for you and the blood of Christ shed for you."

In the hidden uncertainty of our self-worth, when we've wondered if there really could be a place for us at God's Table, you said, "Come and eat. This is the body of Christ broken for you and the blood of Christ shed for you."

In the crucible of transformation when life as we'd known it had fallen apart. When we had questioned our identity you said, "Come and eat. This is the body of Christ broken for you and the blood of Christ shed for you."

In the heat of conflict between friends and lovers, in the dying embers of once impassioned relationships, you said, "Come and eat. This is the body of Christ broken for you and the blood of Christ shed for you."

In the center of our fears and longings for new life, different life, sometimes even the old life we've known, you said, "Come and eat. This is the body of Christ broken for you and the blood of Christ shed for you."

In sickness, in body-shattering and mind-numbing sickness, when treatment left us bereft of desire, you said, "Come and eat. This is the body of Christ broken for you and the blood of Christ shed for you."

And now you have me dreaming of a hungry church and a tangible God, of people I have come to know and perhaps to love, walking to the Table, laying down their burdens for just a moment, daring themselves to dream of healing and reconciliation, daring to think of opening their hearts a little more, their minds, and their hands. Daring to be nourished for another leg of the journey.

These are our bodies, given to you.

About the Author

The author pictured with
Clark Michael Rivinoja (1979–2008)

ENUMA OKORO blogs at reluctantpilgrim.wordpress.com. A freelance writer, Enuma also is a passionate retreat and workshop leader. She graduated from Duke University Divinity School in Durham, North Carolina, and previously served as director of the Center for Theological Writing there. She is co-author, with Shane Claiborne and Jonathan Wilson-Hartgrove, of *Common Prayer: A Liturgy for Ordinary Radicals* (Zondervan, 2010).

Find out More about

FRESH AIR BOOKS®

www.freshairbooks.com

MUD AND POETRY: *Love, Sex, and the Sacred* by Tyler Blanski
  ISBN 978-1-935205-07-4 $12

ANGER: *Minding Your Passion*
  ISBN 9778-1-935205-08-1 $12

HOPE: *It's More Than Wishful Thinking*
  ISBN 978-1-935205-08-1 $12

COMPASSION: *Thoughts on Cultivating a Good Hear*t
  ISBN 978-0-8358-9955-0 $12

FORGIVENESS: *Perspectives on Making Peace with Your Past*
  ISBN 978-0-8358-9956-7 $12

52 WAYS TO CREATE AN AIDS-FREE WORLD by Don Messer
  ISBN 978-1-935205-04-3 $9.95

THE CHOCOLOATE-COVERED UMBRELLA:
  Discovering Your Dreamcode   by Tilda Norberg
  ISBN 978-1-935205-02-9 $14.95

WOMAN OVERBOARD: *How Passion Saved My Life* by Jo Kadlecek
  ISBN 978-1-935205-06-7 $17.95

TALK THAT MATTERS: *30 Days to Better Relationships*
  by Susan Lee Lind & Ben Campbell Johnson
  ISBN 978-1-935205-03-6 $15.95

THE MINDFUL MANAGER: *The God Factor at Work* by Patricia Wilson
  ISBN 978-1-935205-05-0 $18.95